GRAPHIC PROGRAMMING

HP Saturn Assembly Language

By Marcos Navarro

For HP49G, HP49G+ and HP50G Calculators

GRAPHIC PROGRAMMING
HP Saturn Assembly Language
For HP49G, HP49G+ and HP50G Calculators

First Edition

© 2024 Marcos Navarro

While every effort has been made to ensure the accuracy of the information presented in this book, the author makes no warranties, expressed or implied, and disclaims any liability for errors or omissions. The reader assumes full responsibility for the use of this information.

ISBN: 9798310527478

INTRODUCTION

This book is the product of several months of research, during which I have gathered a wealth of information about both the graphics hardware and software incorporated in various models of calculators developed by Hewlett-Packard.

This document fills a significant gap in the literature, addressing a topic rarely covered in depth. My aim is to share the knowledge and experience I've gained with others.

Graphics programming in HP Saturn Assembly Language has a certain degree of complexity, so we have chosen to approach it with a fundamentally didactic focus, trying to make its study and understanding easier and more effective.

One of the greatest advantages of programming in assembly language is the immense number of options when solving a problem. For this reason, after having a good understanding of each topic, the reader will be able to develop new methods on their own, which may even be more efficient than those presented here.

The book is mainly aimed at programmers with a good foundation in *HP Saturn Assembly.* but who want to expand their knowledge of *Graphics Programming* . If you do not have knowledge of this low-level language, it is recommended that you first study the following manual: "*Introduction to Saturn Assembly Language*" by Gilbert Fernandes and Eric Rechlin. You can download it for free at: www.hpcalc.org

It is our hope that these pages will provide readers with an enriching and engaging experience, stimulating their curiosity and nurturing their creative potential.

CONTENT

CHAPTER 1
PRELIMINARY NOTIONS

1.1 The HP Saturn microprocessor

Many models of pocket computers and calculators developed by *Hewlett-Packard* contain an *HP Saturn* microprocessor. This sophisticated electronic device is responsible for processing information, making decisions and executing the tasks we assign to it.

Iconic models such as the HP71B, HP28, HP48S/SX, HP48G/G+/GX and HP49G use one of the different versions of the *HP Saturn* processor as their electronic brain. This means that, although they are machines with different characteristics, they also have many others in common, especially those related to the most fundamental aspects of their internal operation.

In the latest models of RPL graphing calculators, such as the HP49G+, HP48GII and HP50G, where a physical *HP Saturn* chip is no longer available, this processor has been emulated at the software level, in order to take advantage of the enormous number of programs, documents and knowledge that had been developed over the years for previous models.

1.2 When to use Assembly Language?

Developing a very large and complex program entirely in *Assembly Language* can require a lot of time and effort. Many programmers have written programs 100% in *HP Saturn Assembler,* but It should be enough in most cases just use it for those most critical parts of an application, where any improvement in the efficiency of a routine can have a large impact on the performance of our program, which makes any effort we dedicate to optimizing those parts of the code worthwhile.

In other cases, we encounter problems that we cannot properly solve with high-level languages, and we need greater access to *System* resources and tools. So, to achieve our goal we make use of the power of *Assembly Language* programming.

1.3 Why study this language?

There are many possible answers to this question:
- a) Because you like challenges.
- b) Because it's interesting.
- c) Out of curiosity.
- d) Because it's entertaining.

e) Because you want to improve your program.

f) It's something you've wanted to do for a long time.

1.4 Resources needed

For all examples presented in this book we will use the MASD compiler notation, which is included in the HP 49, 49G+ and 50g calculators.

The MASD manual is essential for this book. It's included in the *"HP 50g Advanced User's Reference Manual"*, 2nd Edition (pages 6-11 to 6-42), which you can download for free at:

https://www.hpcalc.org/details/7141

Another very useful resource is the *"HP49G Entry Reference"* by Carsten Dominik, Thomas Rast and Eduardo M. Kalinowski. This document contains a comprehensive catalog of entry points, which were compiled from various sources.

To edit our source code directly in the calculator we can use the powerful Emacs editor, available at:

https://www.hpcalc.org/details/3940

For the purposes of this book, it is recommended that you enable flags -71, -86 and disable flag -92 on your calculator, which are used by the Development *Library* available onIn the previous chapter we learned how to draw graphics on the Screen calculators and which we will use throughout this book.

-71: When enabled, the disassembler suppresses the display of extra memory addresses in the generated code. This setting is crucial to successfully reassemble any generated code.

-86: When enabled, the development library is automatically attached after a warm start event.

-92: When enabled, the MASD assembler defaults to using *System RPL mode* instead of standard *Assembly Language* mode.

1.5 Edit Graphic Objects on a PC

For large graphic programming projects it is very useful to have a tool to edit *Graphic Objects* on the PC. One such editor is *"CPEdit"* developed by Tobias Holgers.

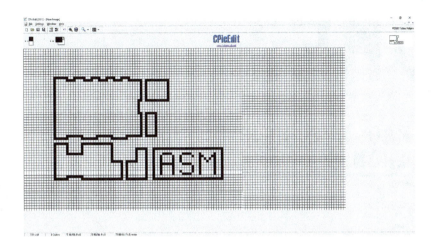

This tool even allows you to edit *Grayscale* graphics:

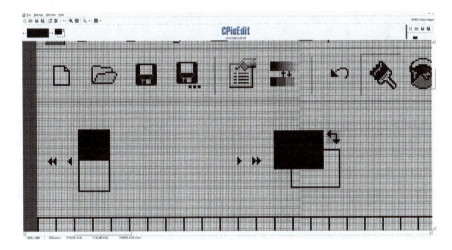

You can download CPicEdit at: https://www.hpcalc.org/details/3837

1.6 Graphic Objects or Grob

With the release of the HP 48S/SX, a new type of *RPL Object* was introduced: the *Graphic Object* (or Grob). This object is used to encode images that can be displayed on the calculator's *Screen*. The Grob became the standard for image encoding on subsequent HP graphic calculators, such as the 48G/G+/GX, 49G, 49G+, 48GII, and 50G. [see *HP Journal*, June 1991, p.17-18]".

The images displayed on your graphic calculator's *Screen* are composed of a grid of tiny squares. Each of these tiny squares is a pixel. A pixel is the smallest individual point in a digital image. The word "pixel" is a contraction of "picture element.

1.7 Internal representation of a Grob

Every image displayed on the calculator *Screen* is stored in the device's memory as a *Graphic Object*, represented by a sequence of hexadecimal digits. Like all *RPL Objects*, the data for a *Graphic Object* is stored contiguously in memory, with each nibble occupying a different memory address.

Address 1	Address 2	Address 3	Address 4	Address 5	...	AddressK
nibble1	nibble2	nibble3	nibbles4	nibble5	...	nibbleK

The first five nibbles, i.e. those at the lowest memory addresses, constitute the **Prolog** of the *Graphic Object*. This number is very special, since all RPL objects of the same type have the same *Prolog value.* For all *Graphic Objects,* the Prolog is **02B1E.**

The next five nibbles after the *Prolog* contain the *Size* of the *Graphic Object.* This is just the number of nibbles the grob occupies in memory, not including the five nibbles of the *Prolog.*

Prolog	Size	N Rows	N Columns	Bitmap
5 nibbles	5 nibbles	5 nibbles	5 nibbles	n nibbles

Next, there is the *Number of Rows* (*N Rows)* and the *Number of Columns* (*N Columns*), encoded with five nibbles for each one.

The final component is the *Bitmap*. Here, each pixel of the Grob is stored as a single bit in memory. A one represents an active (or 'on') pixel, and a zero represents an inactive (or 'off') pixel.

The extension of the *Bitmap* will depend on the size of the graphic.

We can also represent the structure of a *Graphic Object* using a vertical diagram like the following:

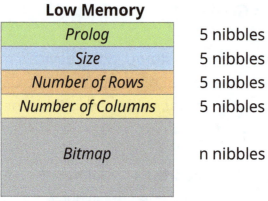

Low Memory

Prolog	5 nibbles
Size	5 nibbles
Number of Rows	5 nibbles
Number of Columns	5 nibbles
Bitmap	n nibbles

High Memory

The part of a *Graphic Object* that is located before the *Bitmap* is named *Header,* and it is made up of the *Prolog, Size, Number of Rows* and *Number of Columns.* The *Header* always occupies 20 nibbles.

Example: Let's draw a rectangle 8 pixels wide by 5 pixels high, using the tool available in the calculator.

When placing the *Graphic Object* on the stack we will see:

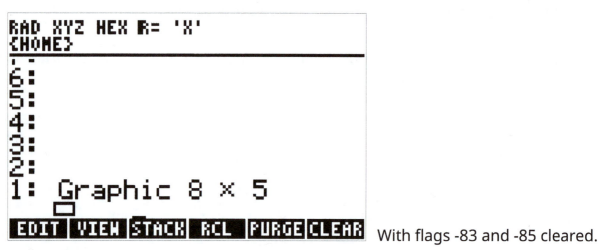

With flags -83 and -85 cleared.

8

With flags -83 and -85 set.

In this last representation, named *Command Line Form,* we can see the following data:

GROB 00014 50000 80000 FF181818FF

This sequence of letters and numbers contains information about the *Graphic Object* at level 1 of the stack:

GROB: Graphic Object.

The numbers that appear next are hexadecimal digits:

00014:	Size minus 10	*Number of nibbles* minus 10.
50000:	Height in pixels	(-> 00005)
80000:	Width in pixels	(-> 00008)
FF181818FF:	Bitmap	(-> FF818181FF)

It should be noted that some data is placed in memory in reverse order, meaning data on the right appears on the left.

The *Bitmap* contains the information about which pixels are set and which are unset. Let's see in detail how the *Bitmap* of a *Graphic Object* is encoded:

Internally, each set pixel is represented by a one, while each unset pixel is represented by a zero.

PIXEL	STATE	BIT
⬛	Set	1
⬜	Unset	0

Each group of four pixels forms a data nibble (4 bits of data) and is represented internally by a hexadecimal digit. But in this encoding, the bits appear in reverse order (R-BITS).

Let's take a look at the following group of four pixels:

PIXELS

The first pixel is set, while the other three are unset. If we represent each set pixel by a one and each unset pixel by a zero, and write them side by side like pixels on the *Screen,* we have:

1000   **BITS**

But, in its internal representation this sequence appears in inverted order, that is, the bits appear organized in the opposite order, like the reflection of an image in front of a mirror. If we have "bit3 bit2 bit1 bit0", it will be encoded as "bit0 bit1 bit2 bit3". In the case of the previous sequence (1000) we will then have:

0001   **R-BITS**

Additionally, the nibble is usually represented in hexadecimal notation:

1h   **NIBBLE**

In the following table we can see all the possible cases for a group of four bits and its *Internal Encoding*:

PIXELS	BITS	R-BITS	NIBBLE
	0000	0000	0h
	1000	0001	1h
	0100	0010	2h
	1100	0011	3h
	0010	0100	4h
	1010	0101	5h
	0110	0110	6h
	1110	0111	7h
	0001	1000	8h
	1001	1001	9h
	0101	1010	Ah
	1101	1011	Bh
	0011	1100	Ch
	1011	1101	Dh
	0111	1110	Eh
	1111	1111	Fh

Now let's go back to the first example, where we had the *Graphic Object:*

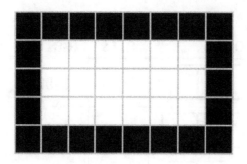

Whose representation in the *Command Line* is:

GROB 00014 5000080000FF181818FF

If we represent pixels using 0s and 1s (BITS) we would have:

Row 1 LCD: 1111 1111
Row 2 LCD: 1000 0001
Row 3 LCD: 1000 0001
Row 4 LCD: 1000 0001
Row 5 LCD: 1111 1111

But, in memory, the bits of each nibble are always encoded in reverse order (R-BITS), meaning that the bits that are furthest to the right appear furthest to the left:

Row 1 mem: 1111 1111
Row 2 mem: 0001 1000
Row 3 mem: 0001 1000
Row 4 mem: 0001 1000
Row 5 mem: 1111 1111

If we represent the value in hexadecimal notation (where each hexadecimal digit represents 4 bits), it is:

Row1: F F
Row2: 1 8
Row3: 1 8
Row4: 1 8
Row5: F F

In memory, these digits are one after the other:

Row1 Row2 Row3 Row4 Row5= FF181818FF

This is the *Bitmap* of our *Graphic Object*!

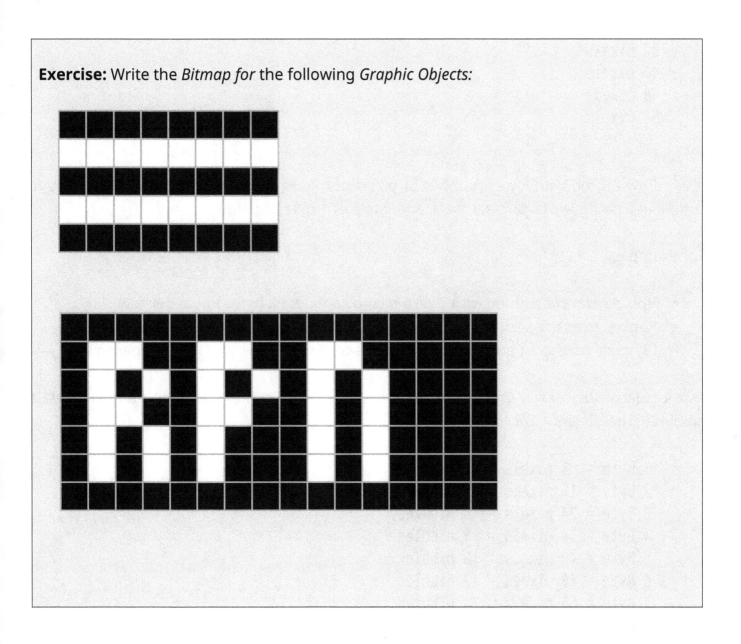

Exercise: Write the *Bitmap for* the following *Graphic Objects:*

1.8 Grobs and bytes

A very important aspect of *Graphic Objects* is that their *Rows* are always encoded in bytes. This means that the number of pixels in a *Row* is always a multiple of 8:

```
 8 pixels
16 pixels
24 pixels
32 pixels
40 pixels
48 pixels
56 pixels
...
```

If we draw a grob with lower number of pixels per *Rows, The System* will pad with zeros to complete a multiple of 8 pixels, that is, a multiple of 1 byte of data.

For example:

- 6-pixel rows are padded with 2 zero bits to complete a byte (1 byte per row).
- 12-pixel rows are padded with 4 zero bits to complete a byte (2 bytes per row).
- 131-pixel rows are padded with 5 zero bits to complete a byte (17 bytes per row).

As a result of the above, *Grobs* or *Graphic Objects* always contain an even number of data nibbles in their *Internal Encoding*:

```
 1 Byte =  8 pixels =  2 nibbles
 2 Byte = 16 pixels =  4 nibbles
 3 Byte = 24 pixels =  6 nibbles
 4 Byte = 32 pixels =  8 nibbles
 5 Byte = 40 pixels = 10 nibbles
 6 Byte = 48 pixels = 12 nibbles
 7 Byte = 56 pixels = 14 nibbles
 8 Byte = 64 pixels = 16 nibbles
 9 Byte = 72 pixels = 18 nibbles
10 Byte = 80 pixels = 20 nibbles
...
```

Example: In the following *Graphic Object,* the *Rows* contain 13 pixels, that is, 3 pixels are missing to complete 2 bytes. *The System* will complete the 2 bytes by filling the remaining bits with zeros. The grob is encoded as:

E1B20 B2000 70000 D0000 FFF1 9991 5551 9951 5D51 5D51 FFF1

Let's see the *Bitmap Row* by *Row:*

Row 1: 1111 1111 1111 1
Row 2: 1001 1001 1001 1
Row 3: 1010 1010 1010 1
Row 4: 1001 1001 1010 1
Row 5: 1010 1011 1010 1
Row 6: 1010 1011 1010 1
Row 7: 1111 1111 1111 1

We note that three zeros must be added to each *Row* to complete 2 bytes. Which results in:

Row 1: 1111 1111 1111 1000
Row 2: 1001 1001 1001 1000
Row 3: 1010 1010 1010 1000
Row 4: 1001 1001 1010 1000
Row 5: 1010 1011 1010 1000
Row 6: 1010 1011 1010 1000
Row 7: 1111 1111 1111 1000

Each group of 4 bits forms a nibble. To obtain the hexadecimal expression we must **read the bits of each nibble from left to right:** for example 1000 must be read as 0001. Applying this to all digits we have

```
Row 1: 1111 1111 1111 0001 = F F F 1
Row 2: 1001 1001 1001 0001 = 9 9 9 1
Row 3: 0101 0101 0101 0001 = 5 5 5 1
Row 4: 1001 1001 0101 0001 = 9 9 5 1
Row 5: 0101 1101 0101 0001 = 5 D 5 1
Row 6: 0101 1101 0101 0001 = 5 D 5 1
Row 7: 1111 1111 1111 0001 = F F F 1
```

So the grob *Bitmap,* written in hexadecimal notation will be:

FFF1 9991 5551 9951 5D51 5D51 FFF1

[We have placed spaces for better understanding, but internally there is no space between the hexadecimal digits.]

To complete the *Internal Encoding* of the grob, we must add three more elements:

Prolog	= 02B1E	
Size	= Total nibbles - 5	*See Note below.*
	= (20+4x7)-5 = 43d	*In decimal notation.*
	= 2Bh = 0002B	*In hexadecimal notation.*
Number of Rows	= 7d = 7h = 00007	
Number of Columns	= 13d = Dh = 0000D	

All these numbers appear in reverse order in memory, that is:

Prolog	--> E1B20
Size	--> B2000
Number of Rows	--> 70000
Number of Columns	--> D0000

Therefore, our Grob will be internally encoded as:

E1B20 B2000 70000 D0000 FFF1 9991 5551 9951 5D51 5D51 FFF1

The completion of the bytes (adding zeros) is closely linked to the operation of the hardware, which when reading the *Bitmap data* always does so in bytes.

Note:

The total number of nibbles occupied by a *Graphic Object* in memory is equal to the sum of the nibbles in the *Header* plus the nibbles in the *Bitmap*. The *Size* of the *Graphic Object* is the space it occupies in memory not including the five nibbles in the *Prolog*.

Exercise: For each grob, determine:
   a) *Width* and *Height* in pixels.
   b) *Size* in nibbles.
   c) *Bitmap* in binary notation.
   d) *Internal Encoding* that represents it.

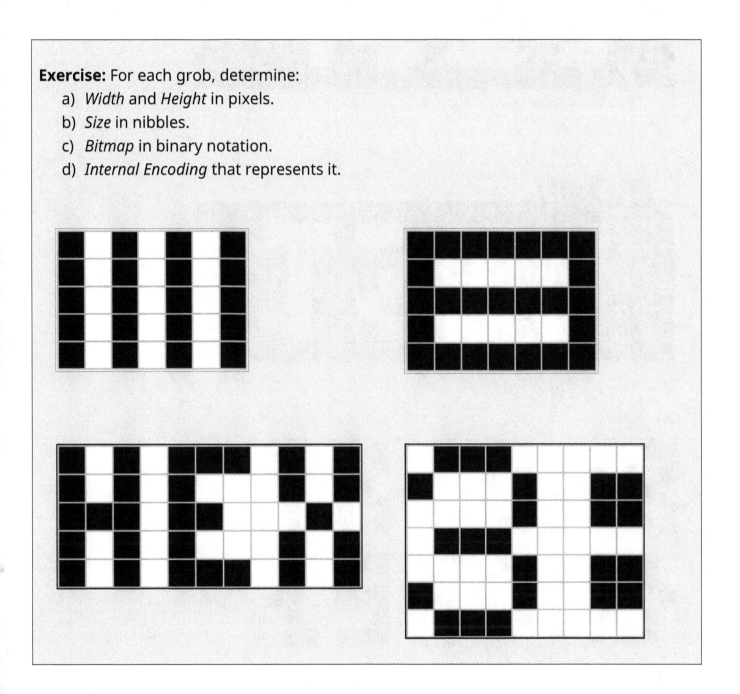

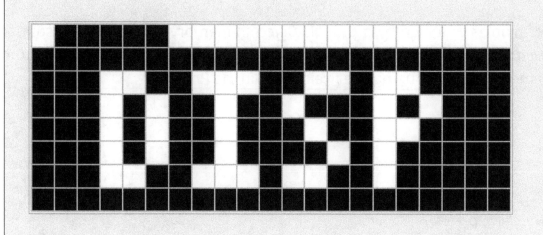

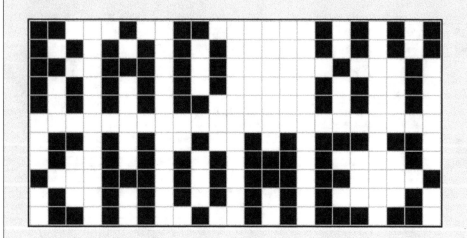

Exercise: For each encoded grob, determines
a) *Width* and *Height* in pixels.
b) *Size* in nibbles.
c) *Bitmap* in binary notation.
d) Draw on the grid.

1) E1B20 B3000 B0000 F0000 FFF7 1004 54F4 5415 5415 D7F4 5414 5414 5414 1004 FFF7

2) E1B20 33000 90000 F0000 FFF7 1004 55D5 5515 9884 5944 59C5 1004 FFF7

3) E1B20 34000 D0000 D0000 FFF1 1001 1E01 1A01 1B11 1B11 9B31 9B31 DF71 DF71 DF71 1001 FFF1

4) E1B20 B3000 B0000 01000 0510 8FF1 9049 FE5F 9049 8FF1 0810 2C34 8FF1 AA25 8FF1

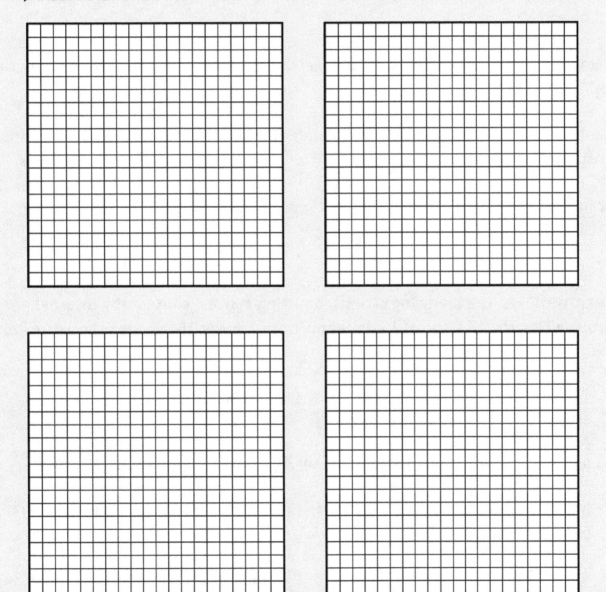

Experimentation

Compiling and decompiling Graphic Objects.
(HP49G, HP49G+ and HP50G)

The *Development Library,* available on the HP 49G/49G+/50G calculators, offers two powerful commands for exploring the *Internal Encoding* of objects:

→H   Given a *RPL Object* on the stack, returns a string with the *Internal Encoding* of a object.

H→   Given a string with the *Internal Encoding* of an object, returns the corresponding object.

Remember that you can attach the *Development Library* by running the following program:
256 ATTACH

By enabling the –86 flag, you ensure that this Library is attached automatically after each warmstart.

You can access the menu of this important *Library* by running:
256 MENU

Experiment 1A: **The following strings, omitting spaces, contain the internal encoding of *Graphic Objects.* Use the H→ command from *Library* 256 to get the corresponding Grobs.**

1) "E1B20 B3000 B0000 F0000 FFF7 1004 54F4 5415 5415 D7F4 5414 5414 5414 1004 FFF7"

2) "E1B20 33000 90000 F0000 FFF7 1004 55D5 5515 9884 5944 59C5 1004 FFF7"

3) "E1B20 34000 D0000 D0000 FFF1 1001 1E01 1A01 1B11 1B11 9B31 9B31 DF71 DF71 DF71 1001 FFF1"

4) "E1B20 B3000 B0000 01000 0510 8FF1 9049 FE5F 9049 8FF1 0810 2C34 8FF1 AA25 8FF1"

Note: We have added some spaces between digits to make the data easier to read, but they should not be included in the string on which the **H→** command will be executed.

Experiment 1B: Draw *Graphic Objects* with the given *Width* and *Height*, using the tool available in the calculator, and use the →H command to obtain their internal encodings:

    1) 4 x 3 pixels.
    2) 6 x 3 pixels.
    3) 8 x 3 pixels.
    4) 9 x 3 pixels.

Hardware
The Yorke chip

The *HP Saturn* processor is found, among other devices, inside the Yorke chip, which is present in the HP48G/G+/GX and HP49G, and is emulated and enhanced in the HP49G+ and HP50G.

The Yorke chip

Below is a photo of the Silicon die inside the casing:

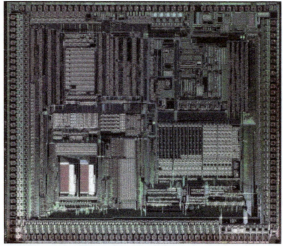

Die of the Yorke.

You can find an interesting collection of photos of the chip at the following link:

https://sites.google.com/view/theyorkechip/home

CHAPTER 2
THE SCREEN GROBS

2.1 Screen Areas.

We can distinguish three areas in the calculator *Screen:*

1) *Indicators* or *Annunciators Area:* Located at the top of the *Screen*, it has six icons that are activated in specific situations to tell the user the status of the calculator.

2) *Secondary Area* or *Menu Area:* It is located at the bottom of the *Screen* and is made up of 8 *Rows* of 131 pixels each.

3) *Main Area:* is the area of the *Screen* that is located between the *Indicators Area* and the *Menu Area.*

2.2 Screen Grobs

Every image displayed on the *calculator Screen* is stored somewhere in the calculator's memory. A *Graphic Object is* required for the *Main Area* of the *Screen,* and other for the *Secondary Area* or *Menu Area.*

We will refer to these *Graphic Objects* as *Screen Grobs* or *Display Grobs.*

For the *Main Area* of the *Screen* the following *Screen Grobs* are available:

- The *Grob for the Graphics Screen* or *PICT Grob.*

- The *Grob for the Texts Screen* or *Stack Grob.*

Only one of these *Grobs* can be displayed in the *Main Area* at a time. The one that is currently displayed is named the *Active Grob.* The remaining *Grob* is named the *Non-Active Grob.*

For the *Secondary Area* of the *Screen* there is the *Menu Grob.*

2.3 Main Area Grobs Registers.

The memory of our calculators contains a series of *Registers*, which are small memory locations that store the addresses of *Screen Grobs*. Each *Register* is identified by its memory address. However, for practical purposes, these addresses are often associated with more easily remembered names or mnemonics.

The address of the *PICT Grob* can be found in the GDISP *Register,* located at address 806E4 in the reserved RAM.

The address of the *Stack Grob* can be found in the ADISP *Register,* located at address 806D5 from reserved RAM.

The address of the *Active Grob* can be found in the VDISP *Register* (also named VDISP1 or SYSUPSTART), located at address 806DA in the reserved RAM. This *Register* may contain either the *PICT Grob* address or the *Stack Grob* address.

The address of the *Non-Active Grob* can be found in the VDISP3 *Register,* located at address 806DF of the Reserved RAM.

Below is a table summarizing the above paragraphs:

Grob for the Main Area of the Screen	*Registers* containing the address of the *Grobs*	
	Address of the Register	**Name of the Register**
Grob for Graphics Screen (PICT Grob)	806E4	GDISP
Stack Grob	806D5	ADISP
Active Grob	806DA	VDISP, VDISP1, SYSUPSTART
Non-Active Grob	806DF	VDISP3

2.4 Secondary Area Grob Register.

The *Menu Grob* address can be found in the VDISP2 *Register,* located at address 806D0 in the reserved RAM.

Grob for the Menu Area of the *Screen*	Registers containing the address of the *Grob*	
	Address of the *Register*	Name of the *Register*
Grob for Menu (*Menu Grob*)	806D0	VDISP2

2.5 Pointer Concept.

A *Pointer Register*, often shortened to "*Pointer,*" refers to a variable containing the memory address of another variable. Therefore, ADISP, GDISP, VDISP, and VDISP2 can be classified as pointers.

If a *Pointer* P contains the address of Q, then P is said to **point to** Q. This is represented by:
     P->Q

Using this notation we can write:

- ADISP-> *Stack Grob*
- GDISP-> *PICT Grob*
- VDISP-> *Activate Grob*
- VDISP2-> *Menu Grob*

2.6 Main Bitmap Registers.

The *Bitmap* of the *Graphic Object* used for the *Main Area* of the *Screen* will be named the *Main Bitmap*. The *Display Controller* requires the memory address of this *Main Bitmap* to know which pixels to set and unset on the *Main Area*.

The *Display Controller* looks for this address in the DISP1CTL *Register,* which is located at address 00120 in the I/O RAM.

There are two very important things regarding this *Register:*

1) If we want the *Display Controller to* display a specific *Graphic Object* in the *Main Area* of the *Screen,* we only have to write the address of its *Bitmap* in the DISP1CTL *Register* (00120).

2) The DISP1CTL *Register* is write-only (W/O), so to access its contents we must do so indirectly, through another *Register* named DISP1CTLg, which contains a copy of its contents. The DISP1CTLg *Register* is located at address 8068D and is sometimes named the *Ghost Register* of DISP1CTL, hence the letter g in its name. This is a very important *Register* and we will use it very frequently throughout the book.

Below is a table summarizing what has been stated in the previous paragraphs:

Registers		DESCRIPTION
Address	**Name**	
00120	DISP1CTL	Contains the address of the *Bitmap* used by the *Display Controller to* know which pixels in the *Main Area* should be set and unset. It is a write-only *Register,* so its contents cannot be accessed directly.
8068D	DISP1CTLg	Contains a copy of the contents of DISP1CTL that we can access. It is sometimes referred to as the *Ghost Register* of DISP1CTL.

2.7 Secondary Bitmap Registers.

The *Bitmap* of the *Graphic Object* used for the *Secondary Area* of the *Screen (Menu Area)* will be named *Secondary Bitmap.* The *Display Controller* needs to have the address of this *Bitmap* in order to know which pixels should be set and unset in the *Menu Area.*

The *Display Controller* looks for this address in the DISP2CTL *Register,* which is located at address 00130 in the I/O RAM.

There are also two very important things regarding this *Register:*

1) If we want the *Display Controller to* display a specific *Graphic Object* in the *Secondary Area* of the *Screen,* we only have to write the address of its *Bitmap* in the DISP2CTL *Register* (00130).

2) The DISP2CTL *Register* is write-only (W/O), so to access its contents we must do so indirectly, through another *Register* named DISP2CTLg, which contains a copy of its contents. The DISP2CTLg *Register* is located at address 806D0 and is sometimes named the DISP2CTL *Ghost Register,* hence the letter g in its name.

Below is a table summarizing what has been stated in the previous paragraphs:

Registers		DESCRIPTION
Address	Name	
00130	DISP2CTL	Contains the address of the *Bitmap* used by the *Display Controller to know* which pixels in the *Menu Area* or *Secondary Area* of the *Screen* should be set and unset. It is a write-only *Register,* so its contents cannot be accessed directly.
80695	DISP2CTLg	Contains a copy of the contents of DISP2CTL that we can access. It is sometimes named the *Ghost Register* of DISP2CTL.

2.8 Special Addresses.

For compatibility purposes, some *Special Addresses* are used to allow access to *Screen Grobs* in an indirect way. The idea is to have an address containing the address of the *Pointers,* so that, even if the address of the *Pointer* changes, the address of its address remains unchanged, increasing the compatibility of the code in different ROM versions.

These Special Addresses are:

```
addrADISP
addrVDISP
addrVDISP2
```

Two nibbles before these addresses we will find the addresses of ADISP, VDISP and VDISP2 respectively; with the small drawback that to retrieve the data, we need to perform "*Double Indirection*".

For example, to point D1 to the Active *Grob Prolog* (VDISP) we do:

```
D1=(5) (=addrVDISP)+2
C=DAT1 A
D1=C
```

We had to "apply indirection twice" to reach the data.

Exercise: Write the program in *Assembly Language* to point D1 to ADISP and VDISP2 using the previous *Special Addresses* addrADISP and addrVDISP2.

```
Answer:
% To point to ADISP:       % To point to VIDSP2:
D1=(5) (=addrADISP)+2      D1=(5)
C=DAT1 A                   (=addrVDISP2)+2
D1=C                       C=DAT1 A
                           D1=C
```

2.9 The D0->Row1 Subroutine.

This *Subroutine* allows D0 to point directly to the *Bitmap* of the *Active Grob*. Recall that the address of the *Active Grob* is found in the VDISP *Register* (also known as VDISP1 or SYSUPSTART), located at reserved RAM address 806DA. The *Active Grob* can be either the *PICT Grob* or the *Stack Grob*.

30

This *Instruction* is called with a GOSBVL:

```
GOSBVL       =D0->Row1
```

If you are using the MASD compiler, you can replace the above line with its equivalent SCREEN, which is easier and faster to type. The compiler will replace the word SCREEN with its equivalent when the code is compiled.

Let's see in detail what this *Subroutine* does:

```
% D0->Row1
RSTK=C
D0=806DA          % D0->VDISP (also named SYSUPSTART and VDISP1).
A=DAT0 A          % A = Active Grob address.
P=0
LC 00014          % 14h = 20d, to skip the first 20 nibbles.
SETHEX
A=A+C A
C=RSTK            % C Register is restored.
D0=A              % D0 point to Active Grob Bitmap.
RTNCC             % Exits the Subroutine and disables the Carry.
```

2.10 Loading a Grobs on the Screen.

To load a *Graphic Object* onto the *Screen,* simply provide the *Display Controller* with the address of its *Bitmap*. This is done by copying the address of the *Bitmap* to *Register* DISP1CTL (00120). This change remains in effect after returning control to RPL and is reverted upon error or calculator reset.

Example: Write a program in *HP Saturn Assembly Language* that takes a *Graphic Object* from the stack and loads it temporarily into the *Screen.* The given object will be 131 x 64 pixels and it will be given at level 1 of the stack:

```
CODE
SAVE

A=DAT1 A
D1=A
D1+10
D1+10
AD1EX
```

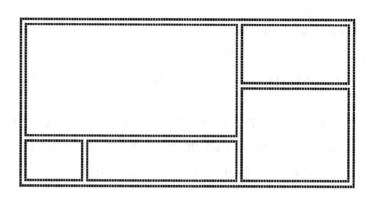

```
D0= 00120        % DISP1CTL
DAT0=A A

LOAD
RPL
ENDCODE
@
```

You can restore the *Screen* to its normal state by restarting the machine with ON+C.

Note:

Sometimes, when taking a *Graphic Object* from the stack and give It's address to the *Display Controller,* the said *Graphic Object* is not displayed correctly centered. This is because the grob is not located at an even memory address. This topic will be discussed in detail later.

Example: Write a code to displays the *PICT Grob* on the *Screen:*

```
CODE
SAVE

D1=806E4          % D1->GDISP
A=DAT1 A          % C = address of PICT Grob.

D1=A
D1+10             % Advance to the PICT Grob Bitmap.
D1+10
AD1EX             % Copy the address of the Bitmap into Register A.

D0=00120          % Point D0 to DISP1CTL.
DAT0=A A
```

```
LOAD
RPL
ENDCODE
@
```

Before running the previous program, draw something in the PICT environment to prevent it from being null.

2.11 Reading data from a Grob on the Stack.

If we have a grob on the *Stack,* we can easily extract parts of its data. As we know, the *Pointer Register* D1 points to level 1 of the *stack,* and therefore, DAT1 will contain the address of the object located there. To access the object, it is enough to apply indirection to the *Pointer.* Then we can read its data by advancing D1 to the position where the data we need to read is located. Let's see some examples:

Example: Write a code that, given a grob at level 1 of the stack, returns its *Prolog:*

```
CODE
SAVE                 % Save the RPL Pointers (GOSBVL 0679B).
A=DAT1 A             % Read the address of the object in stack level 1.
D1=A                 % Applying Indirection.
A=DAT1 A             % Read the first 5 nibbles of the object, i.e.,
                     % his Prolog.
R0=A A
GOSBVL PUSH#         % Execute the routine PUSH# (06537), which takes a number
                     % given in R0.A and returns it to the stack as a bint.
                     % Also restores saved RPL Points and updates
                     % the Stack Pointer D1 to point to the new object.

A=DAT0 A             % Return to the RPL.
D0+5
PC=(A)
ENDCODE
@
```

This program will return the *Prolog* of any given object at level 1 of the stack.

Example: Write a code that, given a grob at level 1 of the stack, returns its *Size*.

```
CODE
SAVE                    % Save the RPL Pointers (GOSBVL 0679B).
A=DAT1 A                % Read the address of the object in stack level 1.
D1=A                    % Applying Indirection.
                        % Now D1 points to first nibble of the grob.

D1+ 5                   % Increase the Pointer by 5 nibbles, to skip the Prolog.
                        % Remember that the Size is located right after
                        % the Prolog, which has five nibbles.
                        % Now D1 point to Size.

A=DAT1 A                % Read the five nibbles that contain the Size.

R0=A A                  % Copy it to R0.
GOSBVL PUSH#            % Push R0 to level 1 of the stack (GOSBVL 06537).
                        % Remember that it's not necessary to do a LOAD, since
                        % the PUSH# Subroutine does it for us, thus restoring all
                        % the RPL Pointers. Also, PUSH# updates D1 to point
                        % to the new object.

A=DAT0 A                % Return to the RPL.
D0+5
PC=(A)
ENDCODE
@
```

Example: Write a code that, given a grob at level 1 of the stack, returns its *Number of Rows* and its *Number of Columns:*

```
CODE
SAVE
A=DAT1 A                % Now A contains the address of the first nibble of
                        % the grob (@Grob).
D1=A                    % Point D1 to the first nibble of the given grob.
R1=A A                  % Save a copy of D1 in R1. Now R1 = @Grob.
```

```
D1+10                % Advance the Pointer to the five nibbles that contain
                     % the Number of Rows.

A=DAT1 A             % A = Number of Rows.

R0=A A               % Send the Number of Rows to the stack as a bint.

GOSBVL PUSH#         % This PUSH restores the copy of the Pointers that was
                     % created with the SAVE Subroutine above. Also updates D1
                     % to point to the new object now in the level 1
                     % of the stack.

SAVE                 % Saves the new values of the RPL Pointers. Remember that
                     % D1 changed when executing the previous PUSH#.

A=R1 A               % A = @Grob
D1=A                 % Again we point D1 to the first nibble of the given grob.
D1+15                % Advance the Pointer to the Number of Columns.
A=DAT1 A             % A= Number of Columns.

R0=A A               % Send the Number of Columns to the stack as a bint.
GOSBVL PUSH#

A=DAT0 A             % Restore the updated RPL Pointers.
D0+5
PC=(A)
ENDCODE
@
```

Exercise: Write code to returns the first five nibbles of the *Bitmap* by pushing them onto the stack.

Exercise: Write a code to returns the *Size, Number of Rows, Number of Columns* and the first 5 nibble of the *Bitmap*, by pushing them onto the stack.

Experimentation
Using the Debugger to Explore Registers.
(HP49G, HP49G+ and HP50G)

Experiment 2A.

Let's analyze the data stored in the ADISP, GDISP, VDISP3, and DISP1CTLg *Registers* to understand how they are related. Before we move on, let's take a moment to review some fundamental concepts

806D0 (ADISP)	Contains the address of the *Stack Grob.*
806E4 (GDISP)	Contains the address of the Grob for *Graphics Screen* or *PICT Grob.*
806DA (VDISP)	Contains the address of the *Active Grob.* This may also be referred to as VDISP1 and SYSUPSTART.
806DF (VDISP3)	Contains the address of the *Non-Active Grob.*

For the *Main Area of the Screen,* the *Controller* looks for the data at the address given in *Register* 00120 (DISP1CTL) of the I/O RAM. This is a Write Only *Register* (W/O), so to access its content we must do it indirectly, through a copy that *The System* saves at address 8068D (DISP1CTLg). This last *Register* is sometimes named the *Ghost Register* of DISP1CTL.

Using a *Debugger,* such as the one in *Jazz* 50g, we will follow the next code to observe the values of all the *Registers* described in the previous paragraphs:

```
CODE
SAVE
A=0 W
B=0 W
C=0 W
D=0 W
R0=A W
R1=A W
R2=A W
R3=A W
```

```
        R4=A W

        D0= 8068D   % D0->DISP1CTLg
        C=DAT0 A    % C = Bitmap address for the Main Area of the Screen.
        D0=C
        D0-10       % Move the Pointer D0 back to the start of the grob's Prolog.
        D0-10
        AD0EX
        R0=A W

        D0=806DA    % D0->VDISP
        C=DAT0 A    % C = Active Grob address.
        D0=C
        R1=C W

        D0=806D5    % D0->ADISP
        C=DAT0 A    % C = Stack Grob address.
        D0=C
        R2=C W

        D0=806E4    % D0->GDISP
        C=DAT0 A    % C = PICT Grob address.
        D0=C
        R3=C W

        D0=806DF    % D0->VDISP3
        C=DAT0 A    % C = address of the Non-Active Grob.
        D0=C
        R4=C W

        LOAD
        RPL
        ENDCODE
        @
```

The above code loads the addresses of the *Screen Grobs* into *Registers* R1, R2, R3 and R4. In addition, it stores the address of the *Grob for the Main Area* of the *Screen* in R0. To obtain the latter, the code subtracts 20 (#20d= #14h) from the address found in *Register* 8068D (DISP1CTLg).

37

	Prolog	Size	N Rows	N Columns	Bitmap
	<-- 20	<-- 15	<-- 10	<-- 5	<-- [DISP1CTLg]

The following *Screen Capture* illustrates the *Debugger's* state after complete data loading:

```
D9F84 8F2D760
        GOSBVL   =GETPTR
DO:87392/E1B20FEB0005000B3000FFFF
D1:C4F58/000000000000000000000000
A:0000000000000868DE  P:0 ST:A059
B:0000000000000000  0000 0101 1001
C:0000000000087392  H MP        H
D:0000000000000000      RSTR:
R0 = 0:0000000000000868DE     1-4    5-8
R1 = 1:0000000000000868DE     00000 00000
R2 = 2:0000000000000868DE     00000 00000
R3 = 3:0000000000087392     00000 00000
R4 = 4:0000000000087392     00000 00000
```

> **R0** contains the address of the *Grob for the Main Area of the Screen* ([DISP1CTLg]–20).
> **R1** contains the address of the *Active Grob*.
> **R2** contains the address of the *Stack Grob*.
> **R3** contains the address of the *PICT Grob*.
> **R4** contains the address of the *Non-Active Grob*.

As seen in the previews *Screen Capture* of the *Debugger*, the address of the *Grob for the Main Area of the Screen* (**R0**), the *Active Grob* (**R1**) and the *Stack Grob* (**R2**) match. That is, the *Display Controller is* using the *Stack Grob*.

Furthermore, we can observe that the *PICT Grob* (**R3**) match with the *Non-Active Grob* (**R4**).

What happens if we run the above code with PICT being active?

If the above code is executed when the *Graphics Screen* is active, we will observe that the address of the *Grob* used by the *Display Controller* (R0) and the address of the *PICT Grob* will match. Also, the *Non-Active Grob* will now be the *Stack Grob*.

Experiment 2B.

A very interesting thing about the *PICT Grob* is that its *Width* and *Height* can be modified by the programmer. This important graphical space can even be null.

Now, we will conduct an experiment to determine PICT's internal state when it is null:

There are two ways to get a null *PICT Grob:*
1) Resetting the calculator with ON-C.
2) Using the *System RPL* KILLGDISP *Instruction.*

We will do it with the second method, compiling and executing the following code:

```
::
        KILLGDISP
;
@
```

Now that PICT is null, let's explore the *Registers* with the following code and the *Debugger:*

```
CODE
SAVE

A=0 W          % Initializing the Registers.
B=0 W
C=0 W
D=0 W

R0=A W
R1=A W
R2=A W
R3=A W

D0=806E4    % D0->GDISP
A=DAT0 A    % A= address of the Grob for Graphics Screen or PICT Grob.

D1=A        % Applying Indirection to point to the PICT Grob.

D1+5        % Skip the Header of the PICT Grob.
D1+15

LOAD
RPL
ENDCODE
@
```

Below is a *Screen Capture* of the Debugger *just* after executing the *Instruction* marked in **blue** in the previous code:

```
D9F7E 174
      D1=D1+   5
D0:806E4/29378 6A37880688853688E964
D1:87392/E1B20 F0000 000000000000000
A:00000000087392  P:0 ST:A059
B:0000000000000000  0000 0101 1001
C:0000000000000000  H MP    8K M
D:0000000000000000      RSTK:
0:0000000000000000   1-4    5-8
1:0000000000000000  00000 00000
2:0000000000000000  00000 00000
3:0000000000000000  00000 00000
4:D7F770881F4C74AD  00000 00000
```

We can notice that D0 contains the address 806E4. This is the address of the GDISP *Register,* which contains the address *of the Grob for Graphics Screen* or *PICT Grob.* Here we find the value 29378. This is the address of the GDISP *Register,* but the digits are in reverse order.

Note that the data always appears in reverse order in memory:

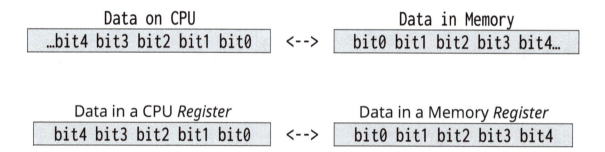

So, by reversing the order of the digits in 29378, we get 87392. We make D1 point to this address, where the *PICT Grob is.* As we can see, the object located there is indeed a *Graphic Object,* since its first five digits (the *Prolog)* are the ones always pressent in this type of *RPL Objects.*

We observe that the *Size* of the *Graphic Object* is F0000, which is 15 in decimal notation. This corresponds to the sum of:

5 nibbles of the *Size*.
5 nibbles from *the Number of Rows*.
5 more nibbles of *Number of Columns*.
0 *Bitmap nibbles*.

Based on the above, we conclude that the null PICT *Grob Bitmap* has 0 nibbles.

Experiment 2C.

Now let's change the *Width* and *Heigh* of PICT and explore the values in the *Registers*. We will expand PICT so that it is 253 pixels wide and 100 pixels high. To do this we will use the following program:

```
::
    BINT253
    BINT100
    MAKEPICT#
;
```

To scan the *Registers* we will use the same code used in Part A.

Below we have a *Screen Capture* of the *Debuguer* after running the code from Part A of the experiment:

The *Prolog, Size, Number of Rows* and *Number of Columns* are marked in the image above. We see that the values correspond to those we had assigned to them, with the only difference being that they are written here in hexadecimal notation:

`46000` -> 00064h = 100d
`DF000` -> 000FDh = 253d

Exercise: Create a *PICT Grob* of any *Width* and *Heigh* you want and explore *the Registers* using a *Debugger*.

Hardware
The Display Control System.

The Yorke chip has a built-in *Display Control System*.

The physical chip, in the HP48 and HP49G, is assisted by two external SED1181FLA chips connected in cascade.

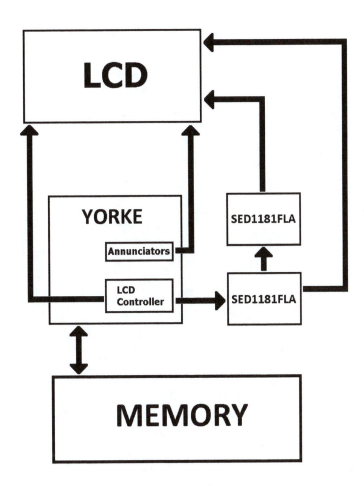

The Yorke chip drives the *Display's 64 Rows,* and 4 of its *Columns;* while the two outer chips drive the remaining *Columns*.

The Yorke also controls the six *Indicators* at the top of the *Screen*.

CHAPTER 3
SCREEN REFRESH

3.1 The Right Margin.

Let's review the *Internal Encoding* of a *Graphic Object*. Suppose we have a *Graphic Object* of 131 x n pixels.

The first 20 nibbles are the *Header* of the *Graphic Object*:

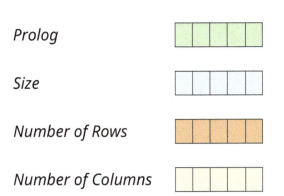

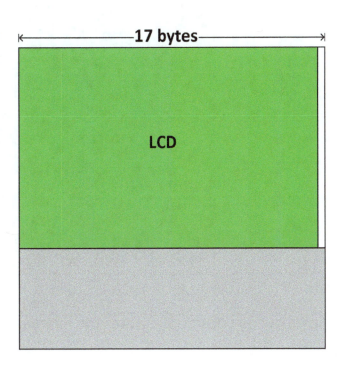

After the *Header*, the *Bitmap* data begins. Each horizontal line of the *Screen* is encoded using 17 bytes. The following scheme illustrates the *Internal Encoding* of this *Graphic Object*:

After the *Header*, the *Bitmap* data begins. Each horizontal line of the *Screen* is encoded using 17 bytes. The following scheme illustrates the *Internal Encoding* of this *Graphic Object*:

The first 17 bytes after the *Header* correspond to the first horizontal line of pixels at the top of the *Screen*, and the last 17 bytes correspond to the last horizontal line at the bottom of the *Screen Area*.

Although 131 pixels are less than 17 bytes, *The System* always encodes the grob in multiples of 8 bits (bytes). Unused bits are padded with zeros. The remaining bits appear as a white stripe in the image above, at the right of the *Liquid Crystal Display* (LCD).

Sometimes, we have a *Graphic Object* whose *Rows* are much longer than the *Screen*. The segment of the *Row* that is after the first 17 bytes is named the *Right Margin* (RM). The following scheme illustrates this case:

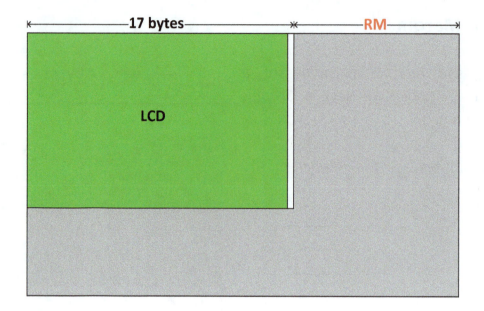

The following scheme illustrates the *Internal Encoding* of this *Graphic Object*:

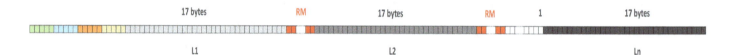

Example: Calculate the *Right Margin for* each *Graphic Object,* given its dimensions.

a) **136** x 80

RM = **Lines Size –** 17 bytes

= CEIL (**136** /8) – 17 bytes

= CEIL (17) – 17 bytes

=17 – 17

= **0** bytes

b) **144** x 64

RM = **Lines Size –** 17 bytes

= CEIL (**144** /8) – 17 bytes

= CEIL (18) – 17 bytes

=18 – 17 bytes

= 1 bytes

= **2** nibbles

c) **159** x 55

RM = **Lines Size –** 17 bytes

= CEIL (**155** /8) – 17 bytes

= CEIL (19.375) – 17 bytes

=20 – 17 bytes

= 3 bytes

= **6** nibbles

Note:

1) The *Lines Size* of a *Graphic Object* is the amount of *Memory Space* that each of its *Rows* uses. This value will always be a multiple of 1 byte, since, as we learned in Chapter 1, the *Rows* are always encoded in even multiples of 1 nibble.

2) The CEIL(X) function returns the positive integer that is greater than or equal to X.

Exercise: Calculate the *Right Margin* for each *Graphic Object,* given its dimensions.
   a) 135 x 64
   b) 146 x 80
   c) 253 x 55

3.2 Screen Refresh (Part I).

Concepts: Display Pointer, Start Address, Secondary Start Address, Right Margin

This section details the *Screen Refresh* process, which is essential for *Graphic Programming* in *HP Saturn Assembly Language*. Be sure to study it carefully.

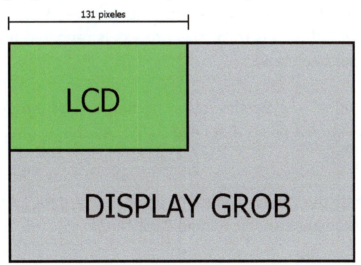

The image on the *Screen* of our calculator is updated periodically. This process is named *Screen Refresh*. This process is performed line by line, starting with the line of pixels at the top of the *Screen*, until it reaches the bottom line.

As we already know, the image data displayed on the *Screen* is a sequence of bits stored in the calculator's memory. A one represents a set pixel, while a cero represents an unset pixel. The *Display Controller* reads this data and updates the pixels according to the *Bitmap* information it finds in memory.

On models such as the HP48S, HP48G and HP49G, the *Screen* is updated 64 times every second. This means that each of its lines is updated 64 times every second. This is done line by line. First the line at the top of the *Screen* is updated, then the one below that, and so on, until reaching the line at the bottom.

A *Pointer,* named *Display Pointer,* indicates the data to be displayed on the *Screen* as *The System* reads it. The data for each line is read 8 bits at a time (byte by byte) and stored in a *Shift Register*.

This process is carried out in two main stages:

In the *First Stage The System* reads the *Grob for the Main Area,* which is located between the *Indicators* and the *Menu Area* (see chapter 2), and in the *Second Stage The System* reads the *Grob for the Menu Area*. We will name *Start Address* the memory address where the *Bitmap* of the *Grob for the Main Area* is located.

The **First Stage** begins by having the *Display Pointer* pointing to the first nibble of the *Main Area Grob Bitmap. The System* reads the first byte of data from the *Bitmap*. The *Pointer* is then incremented by 2 nibbles (1 byte), and the second byte is read. The *Pointer* is incremented again, and the third byte of data is read. This process is repeated until all the data for the first line of the *Screen* has been read.

Now, with this information, *The System* drives the first line of the *Screen*. Driving a line is applying electric voltage to the pixels that needs to be set on that line. With this, those pixels change their color.

The System then updates the *Display Pointer* to point to the data on the second line of the *Screen* by adding the value of a variable named *Right Margin*.

Remember that sometimes the grob is wider than the calculator's *Screen,* so to skip those data that will not be displayed on the *Screen* it is necessary to increase the *Pointer* by a specific amount. That amount is named the *Right Margin*.

The *Right Margin* is the number of nibbles that must be added (or subtracted) to the *Display Pointer* after reading the data of a line, in order to get the *Display Pointer* to point to the first nibble of the data of the next line.

Once this is done, the *Display Pointer* points to the data on the second line and, as with the first line, the data is read and the *Pointer* is incremented, one byte at a time. This process is repeated until all the data for the second line of the *Screen* is read.

Now, with this information, *The System* stops driving the first line and starts driving the second line.

The System then updates the *Display Pointer* again to point to the data on the third line of the *Screen* by adding the *Right Margin* value again.

The above process is repeated until the last line of the *Main Area* of the *Screen* is reached. This last line is then driven, and the *First Stage* of the *Screen Refresh* or *Screen Update* process is completed.

Now we move on to the **Second Stage**, when the *Menu Area* or *Secondary Area of the Screen* is refreshed. For this the *Display Pointer* is loaded with the address of the *Menu Bitmap*. This address is named *Secondary Start Address*. The *Graphic Object* for the *Menu Area* must never be more than 17 bytes wide, since in this *Second Stage* the *Right Margin* offset is disabled and *The System* cannot make adjustments as in the previous stage.

The System starts by reading the first byte at the address indicated by the *Secondary Start Address*, increments the counter and reads the second byte; then increments the counter again and reads the third byte. This process is repeated until the 17 bytes of data in the first line of the *Menu Area* is read.

Now with this information *The System* drives the first line of the *Menu Area* of the *Screen*.

The *Display Pointer* is updated to point to the second line of the *Menu Area* and 17 more bytes are read.

Now *The System* drives the second line of the *Menu Area*.

The above process is repeated until reaching the last line of the *Menu Area* of the *Screen*, thus completing the *Second Stage* of the *Screen Refresh* process.

Upon completion of the *Second Stage*, the sum of *Right Margin* is reactivated and the *Refresh Cycle* is now complete.

This process is repeated continuously.

There are several details that have not been included in this description of the *Screen Refresh* process, but which we will explain later.

Exercise: Answer:
a) What is the first line of the *Screen* to be refreshed? What is the last line?
b) How many bytes of data are typically required for one line of *Screen?*
c) How many bytes are read each time?
d) At what point is the *Right Margin* value added to the *Display Pointer* and why?
e) What does "driving a line" means?
f) What happens to the previous line while data on one line is being read?
g) For what amount of time is each line of the HP49G *Screen* driven?
h) Which area of the Screen *is* updated first?
i) What happens after refreshing the *Menu Area?*

Exercise: Explain what we mean by:
a) *Screen Refresh.*
b) *Display Point.*
c) Right Margin.
d) Stages of the *Screen Refresh* process.
e) Driving a line.

Exercise: Draw a diagram to describes the *Screen Refresh* process as explained in this section.

3.3 Scrolling the Window (Part I).

Concepts: Byte jump

This section explains how to implement *Window Scrolling* in byte increments (even multiples of a nibble).

Since each line on the *Screen* is 131 pixels, and each pixel is represented by a bit in memory, 131 bits would be required for each line, which is 16.375 (131/8) bytes. But the *Controller* is designed to read whole bytes, so it never reads fractions of bytes. So *The System* must read 17 bytes for each line displayed on the *Screen.* Then, the bytes on the line that do not appear on the *Window* are skipped in order to read the data on the next line. This skipping is done by adding the *Right Margin* to *the Display Pointer*.

What if we have a grob whose lines are longer than 17 bytes and we want to *Scroll the Window* **n** bytes to the right? To do this we need to increment the *Start Address* by **2n** nibbles. This increment is shown in the image above by a yellow segment. The red dot, in the upper left corner of the *Screen* in the diagram, represents the new *Start Address.*

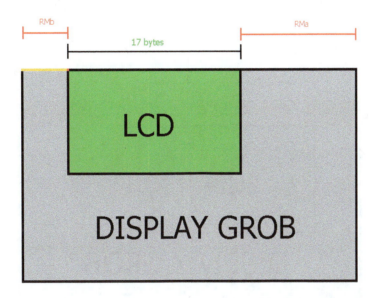

By doing this, the value of the *Right Margin* does not change, since the offset that is discounted at the end of each line is equal to the jump required on the next line to reach the data needed by the *Controller* for the next line of the *Window*.

Right Margin = RMa + RMb

At the end, the jump is perfectly offset.

Exercise: Complete the following table with the missing data:

Display Pointer		Horizontal Window Scrolling (bytes)	
Initial Value	Final Value (Initial Value + **2n**)	Sense (**+ / -**)	Quantity (**n**)
873A6	873A8	to the right	1
87522		to the right	1
87266		to the left	1
87534	87538	to the right	
87812	87800		6
8742E		to the left	8
	8762C	to the right	4
87890	878A2	to the right	

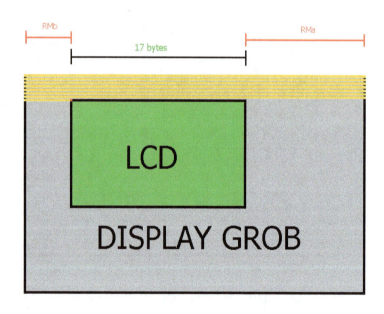

How can we *Scroll the Window* down 7 lines?

Each line of the *Graphic Object* consists of 17 bytes of data plus the *Right Margin:*

    L = 17 bytes + RM

    L = 34 nibbles + RM

So, to jump 7 lines requires adding these 7(34+RM) nibbles to the *Start Address.* This way, the jump is perfectly offset. You can see this jump in the image above, represented by yellow segments. The red dot, in the upper left corner of the *Screen* in the diagram, represents the new *Start Address.*

In general, scrolling the *Window* **m** lines down requires incrementing the *Start Address* by **m (34 + RM)** nibbles.

When scrolling the *Window* up, the calculated offset must be subtracted from the *Start Address.*

Exercise: Complete the following table with the missing data:

Display Pointer		Vertical Window Scrolling (lines)		RM (nibbles)
Initial Value	Final Value [Initial Value + m (34+RM)]	Sense (+ / -)	Quantity (m)	
873A6		Down	1	0
	8758E	Down	3	2
876A0		Up	1	2
877BC	87854	Down		4
87904	879CC	Down	5	
	87B36	Up	4	8
87468	8740C		2	12
87713		Down	5	16

[Answers: 873C8, 87522, 8767C, 4, 6, 87A8E, Up, 87745]

3.4 Screen Refresh (Part II).

Concepts: Left Margin

The *Display Controller* performs a *Left Shift* of the bits of each byte read from memory during the *Screen Refresh* process. This allows the *Window* to be positioned slightly to the right of the *Screen.*

In the previous sections we saw how to perform *Window Scrolling* in multiples of 1 byte (8, 16, 24, 32, ... pixels), but in most cases it is preferred to have less abrupt *Scrolling*.

Left Margin or *BitOffset* is available. This variable can take values between 1 and 7. The value we assign to it will tell the *Display Controller* how many bits to the left it should shift the data after reading it. Then, when the *Screen* line *is* driven, its pixels will appear shifted to the right by the same amount.

When implementing this, it must be taken into account that when the *Left Margin* is greater than three (LM > 3), the *Controller* needs to read 18 bytes instead of 17, in order to correctly perform the *Left Shifting* of the data. This means that, when finishing reading each line, the *Display Pointer* is pointing one byte beyond the appropriate address. The *Display Pointer* must be decremented by two nibbles (1 byte) to achieve the necessary compensation. In the next section we will see how this correction is carried out.

3.5 Scrolling the Window (Part II).

Concepts: *Bits Jumps*

Main ideas:

To *Scroll the Window* to the right on an amount less than 1 byte, that is, from 1 to 7 bits, we use the so-named *Left Margin* (LM). The value that we assign to this variable will indicate to the *Display Controller* how many bits to the left it must shift the read data, thus generating the displacement to the right of the pixels in the *Window*.

One important detail is that when *Left Margin is set to* greater than 3, the *Display Controller* will need to read 18 bytes of data, instead of 17 bytes, in order to process it properly. By doing this, the *Display Pointer* is 1 byte ahead of where it needs to be to read the data for the second line. As a result of this, a small adjustment is required to avoid the image appearing *Misaligned* on the *Screen.*

This *Misalignment* is easily corrected by subtracting this extra byte from the *Display Pointer* when the line data is finished being read. But how can we do that? Easy, through the *Right Margin.* Let's see:

As we know, when the *Display Controller* finishes reading all the data from each line, it adds the *Right Margin* value to the *Display Pointer.* So what we'll do is subtract the extra byte (2 nibbles) from the *Right Margin,* and this way it will then be subtracted from the *Display Pointer* automatically.

We can see this idea expressed in the following equation:

$$(\text{Display Pointer -2}) + \text{Right Margin} = \text{Display Pointer} + (\text{Right Margin -2})$$

3.6 Screen Refresh (Summary).

Below are several tables summarizing the *Screen Refresh* process. In these, we will use the following abbreviations:

DP: *Display Pointer.*
RM: *Right Margin.*
RMd= RM-2
LM: *Left Margin.*
SA: *Start Address.*
SA2:   *Secondary Start Address.*
LC: LINECOUNT (*Lines Counter*).

When $0 \leq LM \leq 3$
STAGE I- Refreshing the Main Area of the Screen:
1) DP = SA is done to point to the beggining of *Bitmap*.
2) DP point to first bit of the current line, that is, the one to be read.
3) One byte of data is read from the line and DP is incremented by two nibbles.
4) The read byte is shifted LM bits to the left (left shift).
5) Repeat steps (3) and (4) until 17 bytes of data have been read.
6) If the *Graphic Object* is 17 bytes wide, DP now points to the first bit of the next line.
7) RM is added to DP. This increment will be zero if the *Graphic Object* read is 17 bytes wide; it will be positive if it is more than 17 bytes wide; or negative if the *Graphic Object read* is less than 17 bytes wide.
8) *Lines Counter* is decreased (LC= LC-1).
9) Steps 2,3,4,5,6,7 are repeated until LC becomes zero. When LC equals zero, stage II of *Screen Refresh begins.*
STAGE II- Refreshing the Menu Area of the Screen:
1) DP=SA2 is done
2) *Offsets (RM and LM)* are disabled.

3) 17x8 bytes of data are read (8 lines of 17 bytes each).
4) *Offsets* are reactivated.
5) The *Screen Refresh Cycle* has been completed.

When $4 \leq LM \leq 7$

STAGE I- Refreshing the Main Area of the Screen:

1. DP = SA is done to point to the beggining of Bitmap.
2. DP point to first bit of the current line, that is, the one to be read.
3. One byte of data is read from the line and DP is incremented by two nibbles.
4. The read byte is shifted LM bits to the left (left shift).
5. Repeat steps (3) and (4) until 18 bytes of data have been read. Note that in this case one more byte is read than in the previous cases.
6. If the *Graphic Object* is 17 bytes wide, DP will now point 1 byte ahead of the first bit of the next line, since it was moved forward 18 bytes instead of 17. To correct this, it will be necessary to subtract 2 nibbles from the RM, obtaining the RMd:

    RMd = RM-2
7. RMd is added to DP.
8. *Lines Counter* is decreased (LC= LC-1).
9. Steps 3,4,5,6,7,8 are repeated until LC becomes zero. When LC equals zero, stage II of *Screen Refresh* begins.

STAGE II- Refreshing the Menu Area of the Screen:

1. DP=SA2 is done.
2. *Offsets* (RM and LM) are disabled.
3. 17x8 bytes of data are read (8 lines of 17 bytes each).
4. *Offsets* are reactivated.
5. The *Screen Refresh Cycle* is now complete.

Exercise: Draw a flowchart describing the process:
    a) When $0 \leq LM \leq 3$
    b) When $4 \leq LM \leq 7$

3.7 The Screen and the Stack Grob.

The HP 48S/SX, 48G/G+/GX and 49G calculators have a display with 131 pixels wide by 64 pixels high, while the HP 50G *Screen* is 131 pixels wide by 80 pixels high.

Although all of these models have the same number of pixels on their *Screens*, the *number of lines* available varies between some of them.

To maintain byte alignment in the *Stack Grob* (as in all *Graphic Objects*), lines must contain a multiple of 8 bits. Thus, for 131 pixels, the following is needed:

```
CEIL (131/8) = CEIL (16.375) = 17 bytes
```

That is, internally each line occupies 136 bits of data (17 x 8), and the bits that are not shown on the *Screen* are filled with zeros to complete the last byte of each line.

Example: How many bytes does the full HP 48 *Screen Bitmap* require? How many bytes are required for the *Menu Area?*

The HP 48G *Screen* consists of 64 lines. And each line requires 17 bytes. Therefore:

```
TotalStack = 64 x 17 = 1088 bytes
```

The *Menu Area* consists of 8 lines of 131 pixels, therefore:

```
TotalMenu= 8 x 17 = 136 bytes
```

Exercise: How many bytes does the 50G *Screen Bitmap* require? How many bytes are required for the *Menu Area?*

Answer:

The HP 50G *Screen.* consists of 80 lines. And each line requires 17 bytes. Therefore:

Total = 80 x 17 = 1360 bytes

The *Menu Area* consists of 8 lines of 131 pixels just like the 48, therefore:

TotalMenu= 8 x 17 = 136 bytes

3.8 The PICT Grob.

Unlike the *Stack Grob,* the *PICT Grob* can have a *Width* or *Rows Size* greater than 131 pixels. This flexibility makes it the ideal graphical space for many projects that require larger *Graphic Objects.*

Logically, the size of the PICT Grob will be limited by the amount of available memory.

In later sections we will work extensively with this important region of memory.

E3 Experimentation
Right Margin and Left Margin Registers.
(HP49G, HP49G+ and HP50G)

Download the *Experimentation Tools* package from the following link:

https://sites.google.com/view/pgsaturn50g/home

Inside the downloaded file you will find several programs designed to help you better understand the topics covered in this book.

For the experiments in this section, follow these steps:

1) Transfer the file **T2.HP** to your calculator.
2) On the calculator, run the RUN file, which is inside the T2 directory.
3) Select the dimensions for the *Background Graphic, and press OK.*

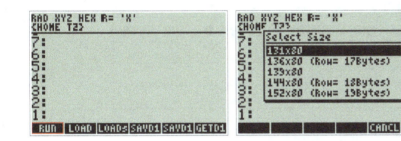 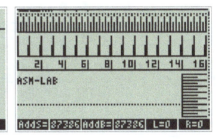

4) You can now modify the *Margins,* while seeing the effects on the *Screen.* This tool can also be used to explore the calculator memory and see the data represented as pixels.

KEY	FUNCTION
X	9 Rows Jump Up.
.	9 Rows Jump Down.
G	32 Rows Jump Up.
J	Jump 32 Rows Down.
H	Jump 64 Rows Up.
K	Jump 64 Rows Down.
Yo	128 Rows Jump Up.
L	Jump 128 Rows down.
UP	1 Row Jump Up.
DOWN	1 Row Jump Down.
LEFT	Jump 1 byte up.
RIGHT	Jump 1 byte down.

<--	Restore the Display Pointer.
TAN	Restores the Display Pointer and Margins (LM and RM).
÷	Reduce Right Margin by 2 nibbles.
*	Increase Right Margin by 2 nibbles.
-	Reduce Left Margin by 1 bit.
+	Increase Left Margin by 1 bit.
R	Reset Right Margin (RM=0).
2	Smart Down.
4	Smart Left.
6	Smart Right.
8	Smart Up.
1	Decreases the Display Pointer by one byte (2 nibbles).
3	Increases the Display Pointer by one byte (2 nibbles).
ON	Exit.

Background Graphic Objects

The *Display Pointer* starts pointing to the *Graphics Screen,* where one of the available *Background Graphics* was previously loaded. The *Graphics Screen* will then have the dimensions of the selected *Background Graphic.* This *Graphic Object* is designed to allow the user to count distances on the *Screen.* It has various scales drawn on it that can be used to measure distances in pixels.

The Menu Area

The *Menu Area* displays information to the user that may be useful in their exploration.

TEXT	DESCRIPTION
AddrS = 8abcd	Graphics Screen address (PICT Grob).
AddrB = 8efgh	Address of the Display Pointer.
L = n	Left Margin (LM) Value.
R = m	Right Margin (RM) Value.

More details:

Note that when you press the **ON** key to exit the graphical environment of the tool, you return to the *Text Screen,* and on the stack there are two binary integers with the values that the *Left Margin* and the *Right Margin* had at the time of exiting.

EXPERIMENTS
Let's conduct some experiments using the T2 *Experimentation Tool*.

Experiment 3A: Left Margin
- Start the T2 tool with the *Background Graphic* of 131x80 pixels.
- Use the **[+]** key to increase the *Left Margin* value, and notice that for every increase of 1 in the *Left Margin,* the *Window* is scrolled one pixel to the right.
- The **[-]** key to decrease the *Left Margin* value and notice that for every decrease of 1 in the *Left Margin,* the *Window* is scrolled one pixel to the left.

Experiment 3B: Left Margin
- Start the T2 tool with the *Background Graphic* of 131x80 pixels.
- Use the **[+]** key to increase the *Left Margin* value to values greater than 3.
- Notice that the image is displayed Misaligned on the *Screen.*

Experiment 3C: Left Margin and Right. Correcting Misalignment
Theory:
- When the *Left Margin* is greater than 3, the *Display Controller* needs to read 18 bytes of data for each *Row* instead of 17, which causes the *Display Pointer* to be one byte ahead of where it should go.

- To correct this problem we must make the *Display Controller subtract the extra byte from the Pointer* address when finishing reading the data from each Row.
- As we know, the *Right Margin* value is added to the *Pointer* after reading each Row. What we will do to correct the *Misalignment* is to assign a negative value of **-2** to the *Right Margin.* This way 2 nibbles (1 byte) will be subtracted from the address after reading each Row, correcting the problem.

Practice:

- Start the T2 tool with *a Background Graphic* of 131x80 pixels.
- Use the **[+]** key to increase the *Left Margin* value to values greater than 3.
- Notice that the image is displayed Misaligned on the *Screen.*
- Now press the **[÷]** key to reduce the *Right Margin* value to **-2.**
- Notice that the *Misalignment* has disappeared.

Experiment 3D: Magin according to the size of the Graphic Object (Part I)

As you have seen, the tool provides different options for the *Background Graphic* to be loaded in the *Graphics Screen.* The dimensions of the *Graphics Screen* will be equal to those of the selected *Background Graphic.*

Start the tool with each of the *Background Graphics* in the table and complete it with the data shown in the *Menu Area* right when it starts. Complete the last question in the last column with a Yes or No.

Background Grob	Left Margin (L)	Right Margin (R)	Is there Misalignment?
131 x 80			
136 x 80			

- Note that for the graphics with 131 and 136 pixel *Width*, the *Right Margin* values match. This is because both graphics are internally encoded with a *Bitmap* of 34 nibbles per *Row*. In the case of a graphic with 131 pixel *Rows*, the remaining bits are padded with zeros to complete the last byte.

> For the grob of 131: CEIL(131/8) = CEIL(16.375) = 17 bytes = 34 nibbles
> For the grob of 136: CEIL (136/8) = CEIL (17,000) = 17 bytes = 34 nibbles

> CEIL(x) *function returns the next integer that is greater than or equal to* x.

- Note that for the graphic with the 131 and 136 pixel *Width,* the *Right Margin* has a value of 0. This is because the *Pointer* does not need to be incremented after reading the data from each *Row,* since they consist of exactly 17 bytes, or 34 nibbles.

    RM0 = 34 - 34 = 0

Experiment 3E: Margin according to the size of the Graphic Objects (Part II)

As you have seen, the tool provides different options for the *Background Graphic* to be loaded in the *Graphics Screen.* The dimensions of the *Graphics Screen* will be equal to those of the selected *Background Graphic.*

Start the tool with each of the *Background Graphics* in the table and fill it with the data shown in the *Menu Area* right when it starts. Complete the last question in the last column with a Yes or No.

Background Grob	Left Margin (L)	Right Margin (R)	Is there Misalignment?
139 x 80			
144 x 80			
152 x 80			

- Note that for the 139 and 144 pixel *Width Graphs the Right Margin* values match. This is because both graphs are internally encoded with a *Bitmap* of 36 nibbles per *Row.* In the *Grob* whose *Rows* are 139 pixels the remaining bits are padded with zeros *to* complete the last byte.

    For the grob of 131: CEIL (139/8) = CEIL (17.375) = 18 bytes = 36 nibbles.
    For the grob of 136: CEIL (144/8) = CEIL (18,000) = 18 bytes = 36 nibbles.

- Note that for the 139 and 144 pixel *Width Graphic Objects,* the *Right Margin* has a value of 2. This is because there is one byte of data (2 nibbles) before the data for the next Row. So *The System* **needs to skip that byte,** which it does by adding the *Right Margin* to the address that the *Pointer has* when it finishes reading the 17 bytes of data for the *Row.*

    RM0 = 34 - 36 = 2 nibbles

- Note that the graphic with 152 pixel *Width* requires a larger *Right Margin* than the two previous graphics:

  For the grob of 136: CEIL (152/8) = CEIL (19,000) = 19 bytes = **38** nibbles.

  RM0 = 34 - 38 = 4 nibbles

Experiment 3F: Adjusting the Right Margin when the Left Margin is greater than 3.
- Start the T2 tool with each of the *Background Graphic.*
- For each case, note the *Right Margin* value that is displayed in the *Menu Area on startup.*
- Use the **[+]** key to increase the *Left Margin* value to values greater than 3.
- When the value of *Left Margin* is greater than 3, the *Screen shows Misalignment.*
- Now use the key **[÷]** to find the value that corrects the *Misalignment.*

Background Grob	Left Margin (L)	Right Margin (R)	
		Initial Value	Value without Misalignment
131 x 80	3 < L ≤ 7		
136 x 80	3 < L ≤ 7		
139 x 80	3 < L ≤ 7		
144 x 80	3 < L ≤ 7		
152 x 80	3 < L ≤ 7		

Note that the difference between the two values is 2 nibbles, or 1 byte. That is the extra byte of data that the *Display Controller* needs to read in order to shift the data more than 3 bits to the left. The *Pointer* needs to be corrected to properly point to the data in the next Row. This is done by subtracting 2 nibbles from the address of the *Pointer.*

Note that after the correction, the image remains without *Misalignment* for any *Left Margin* value greater than 3 (that is, 3 < L ≤ 7). But if we reduce the *Left Margin* to values of 3 or less, the *Controller* stops reading the extra byte, and we will need to return the *Right Margin* to its *Initial Value* to avoid the new *Misalignment.*

Hardware
Screen Connectors.
(HP49G)

Located behind the *Display* is the calculator's motherboard, which houses the Yorke chip and the auxiliary SED1181F *Columns* drivers.

HP 49G's *Motherboard*. In the center we see the Yorke chip.

After removing the *Motherboard,* we find the *Display* and its two *Elastomeric Connectors,* which connect the *Display* to the *Motherboard.*

Rear view of the *Display* showing the *Elastomeric Connectors.*

67

The image below shows the *Motherboard,* focusing on the side with the *Display* terminals. These terminals (highlighted in red) are where the *Elastomeric Connectors* make contact.

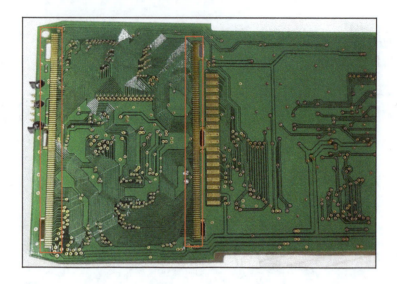

Motherboard connectors that go to the *Display.*

In the following photo, we see a closer view of the *Elastomeric Connector* that connects the *Display* to the *Motherboard* of the HP49G.

In the center, the *Elastomeric Connector.*

CHAPTER 4
THE ANNUNCIATORS

4.1 The Annunciators

At the top of the *Screen* there are six icons named *Indicators* or *Annunciators* that are activated in specific situations to indicate to the user the operating status of the calculator. These *Annunciators* are:

Left Shift: Indicates that the *Left Shift* key was pressed.

Right Shift: Indicates that the *Right Shift* key was pressed.

Alpha: Indicates to the user that the calculator is in text input mode.

Alert: May indicate that the battery is low or that there is a pending alarm.

Bussy: Indicates that the calculator is not ready to process new input.

Transmitting: Indicates to the user that the calculator is transmitting data to an external device.

On the HP48 and HP49G, the Yorke chip directly controls these annunciators via individual pins for each indicator, plus a common pin.

4.2 Annunciators Control Registers.

We have a two-nibble *Register* at address **#0010Bh**, in the I/O RAM area, where we can control all the *Indicators*. This *Register* is usually named ANNCTL. Each pin is controlled by a different bit.

We have also observed experimentally that the most significant bit of the *Register* can deactivate all *Indicators* at once. So, to activate an *Annunciator* two things are required: 1) activate the *Annunciator bit* and 2) that the most significant bit of the *Register* is activated. In this manual we will refer to this last bit as the **AON bit** (Annunciators ON), which is somewhat similar to the DON bit (Display ON).

In the following table we can see the *Indicators* control *Register,* and the *Indicator* associated with each bit of it:

Address	Bit 3	Bit 2	Bit 1	Bit 0
#0010Bh	Alert	Alpha	Right Shift	Left Shift
#0010Ch	Announcers ON		Transmitting	Busy

4.3 Programming the Annunciators.

Below, we will see several examples of codes for programming the calculator's Annunciators or Indicators:

Example: Write a code to activates the *Right Shift Indicator.*

As you can see in the table above, the second bit of the *Register* is the one that controls the *Right Shift Indicator.* Therefore, to activate it we just need to change its value to one.

```
CODE
SAVE
LA 82                    % 82h= 1000 0010
D0=0010B
DAT0=A  B

LOAD
RPL
ENDCODE
@
```

We copy to the *Register* the number **82**h which in binary is "**1000 0010**". The **1** marked in **red** is to activate the **AON** bit, while the **1** marked in **green** activates the **Right *Shift Indicator.*** It must be remembered that the nibbles are inverted when passing from *Register* A to memory, leaving the **8** at the highest address.

Please note that these changes only take effect while our code is running. When we return to the RPL, the *Operating System* will again have control of the *Indicators.* This is why it is necessary to pay close attention to the *Screen* in order to see the effect of our program.

Example: Rewrite the code from the previous example to activate all *Indicators* at the same time.

```
CODE
SAVE
LA BF                    % BFh= 1011 1111
D0=0010B
DAT0=A B

LOAD
RPL
ENDCODE
@
```

Example: Write a code to activates the *Left Shift Indicator,* but without altering the state of the other *Indicators.*

The first example had the limitation that it affects the state of the other bits in the *Register.* We can write a code to activate the bit for *Left Shift,* without modifying the state of the other *Indicators.*

Let's see:

```
CODE
SAVE              % Save RPL Points.
D0=0010B          % Point to ANNCTL.
A=DAT0 B          % Read the ANNCTL Register in A.B.
ABIT=1 0          % To activate the bit for Left Shift Indicator.
ABIT=1 7          % To activate the AON bit.
DAT0=A B          % Update ANNCTL.
LOAD              % Restore RPL Pointers.
RPL               % Return to the RPL.
ENDCODE
@
```

Exercise: Rewrite the code from the previous example to activate the *Right Shift Indicator* without affecting the state of the other *Annunciators.*

Exercise: Rewrite the code from the previous example to activate the *Right Shift Indicator* and the *Alpha Indicator* simultaneously.

Example: Write a code to disable all *Annunciators*.

```
CODE
SAVE              % Save RPL Pointers.
D0=0010B          % Point to ANNCTL.
A=DAT0 B          % Read the ANNCTL Register in A.B.
ABIT=0 7          % To disable the AON bit.
DAT0=A B          % Update ANNCTL.

LOAD              % Restore RPL Pointers.
RPL               % Return to the RPL.
ENDCODE
@
```

Example: Write a code to activate all the *Annunciators* using the *Instruction* ABIT=1 n.

```
CODE
SAVE
D0=0010B
A=DAT0 B
ABIT=1 0
ABIT=1 1
ABIT=1 2
ABIT=1 3
ABIT=1 4
ABIT=1 5
ABIT=1 7
DAT0=A B

LOAD
RPL
ENDCODE
@
```

Exercise: Write a code to activates the *Annunciators* 0, 2, 4, and deactivates the *Annunciators* 1, 3, 5

Example: Write a code to activate the *Annunciators* in sequence.

```
CODE
SAVE
LA 01              % 81h = 1000 0001
LC 06              % Annunciators counter
C-1 B
B=C B

D0=0010B

*LoopX
ABIT=1 7
DAT0=A B
A=A+A B

B-1 B
GONC LoopX

LOAD
RPL
ENDCODE
@
```

In this example, the loop is so fast that it is impossible for us to see the transition from one *Annunciator* to the next. To fix this problem we can add a little extra code to consume some time and creates a delay that allows us to observe the transition. Let's see it in the following example:

Example: Write code to activate the *Annunciators* sequentially. Use a NOP instruction, which consumes processor cycles, to generate a time delay interval for transitioning from one *Annunciator* to the next.

```
CODE
SAVE
LA 01          % 81h = 1000 0001.
LC 06          % Annunciators counter.
C-1 B
B=C B
```

```
D0=0010B

*Loop1
ABIT=1 7
DAT0=A B
A=A+A B
LC 0FFFF
*Loop2
$64000              % NOP5
C-1 A
GONC Loop2

B-1 B
GONC Loop1

LOAD
RPL
ENDCODE
@
```

Exercise: Write code to activate the *Annunciators* in sequence, but in reverse order to the previous example.

Parts of the Liquid Crystal Display.

This diagram shows the different parts of the calculator display:

1- Light Source.

2- Front Polarizer.

3- *Front Panel* or *Rows Panel.*

4- Liquid Crystal.

5- *Rare Panel* or *Columns Panel.*

6- Rare Polarizer.

7- Reflector.

And the:

8- User's eye.

The *Liquid Crystal Displays* consist of, among other things, two Glass *Panels and two Light Polarizers.*

Between the two glass panels there is a very thin layer of a special liquid named *Liquid Crystal,* which is sensitive to electrical fields.

The conductive lines (for *Rows* and for *Columns)* are drawn on the *Panels* using an almost transparent material. This material is very special because it can conduct electricity.

Screen pixel is a point where a line on the *Front Panel* overlaps another line on the *Rare Panel.* These lines never make contact, because they are separated by the *Liquid Crystal,* but they look this way when looking at the *Screen* from the front.

A pixel is set by applying an electrical potential difference to the two lines that pass above and below it. The generated electric field modifies the orientation of the layers of *Liquid Crystal* molecules that are located between the *Panels,* reducing the amount of light that can pass through the *Polarizers.*

This is fascinating technology!

The Light Polarizer

In the following images we can see the two HP48G's *Display Polarizers.* In the image on the right, the area where the *Polarizers* overlap looks dark, while in the image on the right, where the *Front Polarizers* has been rotated, more light passes through , and the interception area looks lighter. A similar effect occurs when a pixel is set on the *Screen.* While here we have done it manually, in the *Screen* this is done by the *Liquid Crystal* molecules, which align differently when a difference in electrical potential is applied to them.

 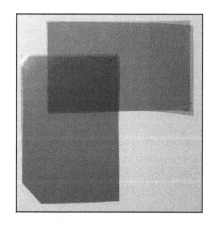

CHAPTER 5
SCROLLING THE WINDOW

5.1 Scrolling the Window (Part II)

As we already know, the HP49G calculator's *Display* has a resolution of 131 x 64 pixels, while the HP 50G's *Display* has a resolution of 131x80 pixels. But sometimes the *Display Controller* is accessing a *Graphic Object* that is larger than the calculator's *Screen* and therefore cannot be displayed completely on the *Screen.* The part of the graphic that we can see at a given time is named the *Window.*

So, when the *Graphic Object* is larger than the calculator *Screen,* we will not be able to see all its points at the same time, but we can *Scroll the Window* to the different areas as needed.

The *Scrolling of the Window* can occur in different ways: we can make a horizontal or vertical displacement, and each of these can be done in two different directions. So we have:

Scrolling the *Window:*

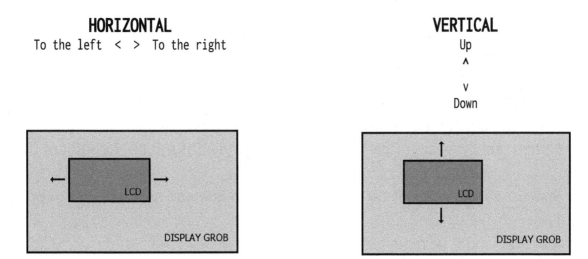

Let's start by analyzing the simplest case, when the *Window* scrolls one byte (8 pixels) to the right. But before we start with that topic, let's review the following:

As we saw earlier, the *Refresh Cycle* normally starts with the *Display Pointer* pointing to the first byte of the *Bitmap.* The *Display Controller* will read 17 bytes, one at a time, incrementing the value of *Display Pointer* as it reads.

After completing the reading of these 17 bytes. *The System* automatically proceeds to add the value of the *Right Margin* to the *Display Pointer,* in order to offset its value to point to the data on the second line.

The System reads 17 bytes from the second line, one byte at a time, and then adds the *Right Margin*.

The process will be repeated until all the lines on the *Main Screen are complete.*

Let's do a thought experiment:

Suppose that, instead of having a *Screen* of 17 bytes per line, we have a *Screen* where each line only takes 5 bytes.

B11	B12	B13	B14	B15	RM	
B21	B22	B23	B24	B25	RM	
B31	B32	B33	B34	B35	RM	
B41	B42	B43	B44	B45	RM	

<----------- 5 bytes ----------->

The *Screen Refresh* process would be as follows:
- The *Display Pointer* initially points to the address of the byte B11.
- *The System* reads 5 bytes of data (instead of 17) and adds the RM to point to the second line.
- *The System* reads 5 bytes of data from the second line and adds the RM to point to the third line.
- This process would be repeated until the data for all lines was read.

If we increase the initial value of the *Display Pointer* by 2 nibbles (1 byte), RM is also reduced by 2 nibbles.

B11	B12	B13	B14	B15	B16	RM-2	
B21	B22	B23	B24	B25	B26	RM-2	
B31	B32	B33	B34	B35	B36	RM-2	
B41	B42	B43	B44	B45	B46	RM-2	

<----------- 5 bytes ----------->

The System will now start reading at B12. But since we have not changed the RM value in the *Display Controller* configuration, it will increment the *Display Pointer* in RM units. That is, the next line will start at B22, the next at B32, and the last at B42.

This would occur for any increment of the initial value of the *Display Pointer,* and it also occurs when we do it on our HP calculator.

We can deduce from the previous analysis that **to scroll the *Window* n bytes to the right,** you just have to increase the initial value of the *Display Pointer* by 2n nibbles. By doing this, it is not necessary to modify the *Right Margin,* since its current value maintains consistency, since when *The System* adds the *Right Margin* at the end of each line read, the *Display Pointer* will continue to point one byte ahead of the address that the line had previously.

Let's see the code:

```
CODE
SAVE
D0=8068D          % DISP1CTLg
A=DAT0 A
D0=A
D0+2              % Point 1 byte ahead
AD0EX

D1=00120          % DISP1CTL
DAT1=A A

LOAD
RPL
ENDCODE
@
```

If the *Screen* is wider than 17 bytes when this code is executed, the *Window* will scroll one byte to the right.

If the current *Screen* is exactly 17 bytes wide, we will see a rotation effect of the *Screen,* 8 pixels to the left.

The *Screen* will return to its previous state when we restart the calculator or when an error occurs. We can also run another code that returns the *Window* to its original position.

To *Scroll the Window* by 4 nibbles (2 bytes) instead of 2 nibbles (1 byte), simply replace the 2 with a 4 in the preceding code:

```
        CODE
        SAVE
        D0=8068D        % DISP1CTLg
        A=DAT0 A
        D0=A
        D0+4            % Point 2 byte ahead
        AD0EX

        D1=00120        % DISP1CTL
        DAT1=A A

        LOAD
        RPL
        ENDCODE
@
```

If we want to *Scroll the Window* to the left instead of the right, we should subtract rather than add. Consequently, the code for a 2-byte displacement to the left is:

```
        CODE
        SAVE
        D0=8068D        % DISP1CTLg
        A=DAT0 A
        D0=A
        D0-2            % Point 1 byte behind
        AD0EX

        D1=00120        % DISP1CTL
        DAT1=A A

        LOAD
        RPL
        ENDCODE
        @
```

Let's now consider a **vertical scroll down**: In this case, we must advance the *Display Pointer* by a line. Remember that a line has 17 bytes plus the *Right Margin*. Also remember that in the code everything must be expressed in nibbles and, therefore, the value to add will be 34 nibbles plus the *Right Margin*.

The code will be:

```
CODE
SAVE

D1=80692          % LINENIBSg.
A=0 A             % Clear A.A.
A=DAT1 X          % Read the value of the Right Margin in A.X.

D0=8068D          % DISP1CTLg.
C=DAT0 A          % Read the address of the Bitmap.
C=C+A A           % Add the Right Margin.
D0=C
D0+34             % Add 17 bytes.
CD0EX

D1=00120          % Update the Start Address of the Display Pointer.
DAT1=C A
LOAD
RPL
ENDCODE
@
```

Exercise:

a) Write code to *Scroll the Window* one line vertically up.

b) Write a code to *Scroll the Window* 8 lines, vertically down using one of the following two methods:

1. Using a loop.
2. By manually calculating the increment value and incorporate that value into the code.

5.2 Scrolling the Window (Part III)

Generally, we want to perform horizontal scrolling that is smaller than 8 pixels (1 byte). For this kind of scrolling we must use the so-named *BitOffset*.

The *BitOffset* corresponds to the value of the first four bits at memory address #00100, in the I/O RAM.

This value is often referred to as the *Left Margin* of the *Screen.*

The *Left Margin* is encoded using 3 bits of data, and It allows us to move the *Window* from 1 to 7 pixels to the right or left.

The fourth bit of the *Register* that contains the *Left Margin* is named the DON bit or Display ON bit. Its state determines whether the *Screen* will be on or off. When the DON bit is zero, the *Screen* will be off; when the DON bit is 1, the *Screen* will be on. The DON bit is always the most significant bit of *the Register.*

Display		*BitOffset (Left Margin)*		Value in Address #00100	
Status	DON bit	Decimal	Binary	Binary	Hexadecimal
ON	1	0	000	1000	8
ON	1	1	001	1001	9
ON	1	2	010	1010	A
ON	1	3	011	1011	B
ON	1	4	100	1100	C
ON	1	5	101	1101	D

ON	1	6	110	1110	E
ON	1	7	111	1111	F

5.3 How does it work?

According to my research, on the original hardware the *Controller* reads the data normally, i.e. 1 byte at a time. But after being read, the data is shifted n bits to the left, according to the *BitOffset* value **n**.

In practice, when we want to *Scroll the Window* **n** pixels to the left, we modify the *Left Margin,* so that its value is **8 + n**. The addition of 8 is to ensure that the DON bit has a value of 1 and the *Screen* remains on.

Even though the DON is a single bit, that bit is in the most significant position of the nibble:

1000 binary = 8 hexadecimal

Example: Write a code to *Scroll the Window* 1 pixel to the left:

```
CODE
SAVE

LC 09       % 9h = 8h + 1h, where 8 is for the DON bit and
            % 1 is for the BitOffset.
D0=00100    % D0->BITOFFSET
DAT0=C 1    % Modify the Left Margin, keeping the Display on.

LOAD
RPL
ENDCODE
@
```

Note:
If we write the hexadecimal #9h in binary notation we have **1001**. We see that this value activates the **DON** bit and at the same time assigns a value of **1**, that is **001** in binary, to the *Left Margin*.

Example: Write a code to *Scroll the Window* n pixel to the left, where n is a binary integer (Bint) given at level 1 of the stack:

```
CODE
% Warning: This code requires a binary integer at level 1 of the stack
% before being executed.

SAVE
A=0 W              % Initializing the Registers to be used.
C=0 W

GOSBVL POP#        % Bint →A.A
                   % Use C.A
                   % Updates RPL Pointers.

D0=00100           % D0->BITOFFSET.
ABIT=1 3           % To have DON bit = 1.
DAT0=A 1           % Modify the Left Margin, keeping the Display on.

LOAD
RPL
ENDCODE
@
```

5.4 When the Left Margin is greater than 3.

As we discussed earlier, in the original hardware the *Display Controller* reads data for each *Row*, one byte at a time. After reading each byte, it shifts the bits to the left according to the *BitOffset* value. The total number of bytes in a *Screen Row* is 17 bytes.

When the *BitOffset* is greater than 3 something very interesting happens: Instead of reading 17 bytes per *Row*, the *Display Controller* needs to read 18 bytes in order to properly perform the *Data shifting*. When this happens, the *Display Pointer* ends up pointing one byte ahead of the address where it should be. As a result of this discrepancy, the image is displayed *Misaligned* on the *Screen*.

The problem is fixed by subtracting 2 nibbles from the value that the *Display Pointer* will have after reading each *Row*.

How can we do this in a practical way? Let's see:

We know that after reading the data from a *Row*, *The System* adds the value of the *Right Margin* to the *Display Pointer*. Therefore, if we subtract those 2 nibbles from the *Right Margin*, they will also be subtracted from the *Display Pointer* after executing the reading of the data from each *Row*.

We will then have two situations: One in which the *Left Margin* has a value between 0 and 3, where the normal value of the *Right Margin* is added; and the other case, when the *Left Margin* has a value between 4 and 7, in which we will decrement the *Display Pointer* by 1 byte (2 nibbles) through the *Right Margin*.

Example: Write code that *Scrolls the Window* 4 bits to the left and corrects the *Display Pointer* so that the data is displayed properly.

```
CODE
SAVE
LA 0C           % Ch = 8h + 4h, where 8 is for the DON bit and 4
                % is for the BitOffset (see Note below).
D0=00100        % D0->BITOFFSET.
DAT0=A 1        % Modify the Left Margin, keeping the Display on.
D1=80692        % D1->LINENIBSg, Right Margin (Read).
C=DAT1 X
C-2   X
```

```
D1=00125          % D1->LINENIBS, Right Margin (Write).
DAT1=C X

LOAD
RPL
ENDCODE
@
```

Note:

If we write the hexadecimal #Ch in binary notation we have **1100**. We see that this value activates the **DON** bit and at the same time assigns a value of **4**, that is **100** in binary, to the *Left Margin*.

Exercise: Rewrite the above code to *Scroll the Window* by 7 bits to the left and correct the *Display Pointer* so that the data is displayed properly. Observe the behavior of the code using a *Debugger*.

Example: Write a code to *Scroll the Window* in **n** pixel to the left, where **n** is a binary integer (Bint) given at level 1 of the stack. When the value of **n is greater than 3**, the *Display Pointer* must be corrected through the *Right Margin* value, so that the data is displayed properly on the *Screen*.

```
CODE
% This code requires a binary integer #n at level 1 of the stack.

SAVE
A=0 A
C=0 A

GOSBVL POP#       % # ->A.A
                  % Use C.A
                  % Updates RPL Pointers.
```

```
D0=00100          % D0->BITOFFSET, Left Margin.
ABIT=1 3          % Making DON bit=1, for Display on.

DAT0=A 1          % Modify the Left Margin, keeping the Display on.
LC 0B             % Bh= 8h + 3h = DON + LM (see Note below).
?A<=C B           % Checking if RM correction is not necessary.
GOYES Exit
D1=80692          % D1->LINENIBSg, Right Margin (Read).
C=DAT1 X
C-2   X
D1=00125          % D1->LINENIBS, Right Margin (Write).
DAT1=C X

*Exit
LOAD
RPL
ENDCODE
@
```

Note:

The hexadecimal value #Bh is equivalent to **1011** in binary notation. We can notice that this value activates the **DON** bit and at the same time assigns a value of **3**, that is **011** in binary, to the *Left Margin.*

Exercise: Combining *System RPL* and *HP Saturn Assembly Language,* write a program to *Scrooll the Window* horizontally, both to the right and to the left, depending on the keys the user press. Use the knowledge acquired in this chapter.

Exercise: Develop a program *to Scroll the window* both horizontally and vertically, using the directions keys. You can combine both *System RPL* and *HP Saturn Assembly Language.* Use the knowledge acquired in this chapter.

Display Controller Registers
(48G/48G+/48GX/ 49G/49G+/50G)

Register		Ghost		Description	Size (nibbles)
Name	**Address**	**Name**	**Address**		
=BITOFFSET	#00100			DON bit & *Left Margin* of GROB.	1
=DISP1CTL	#00120	=DISP1CTLg	#8068D	Contains the address of the *Bitmap* in the *Grob* for the *Main Area of the Screen.*	5
=LINENIBS	#00125	=LINENIBSg	#80692	*Right Margin* of GROB.	3
=LINECOUNT	#00128	=LINECOUNTg	#8069A	*Lines Counter* & *VSYNC.*	2
=DISP2CTL	#00130	=DISP2CTLg	#80695	Contains the address of the *Bitmap* for the *Menu Area.*	5

Note:

The *Right Margin* is encoded in memory using three nibbles, but the least significant bit is ignored by *The System*. Therefore, it always increments the *Display Pointer* by an even number of nibbles, i.e., by a multiple of one byte. Furthermore, the *Right Margin* can have both positive and negative values, allowing additions to or subtractions from the *Display Pointer*.

E5 Experimentation

Smart Window Scrolling.

The *Experimentation Tool* T2 has an *Smart System* for *Scrolling the Window,* which adjusts the *Right Margin* values as we increase the *Left Margin.*

When we increase the *Left Margin* to a value greater than 7 (that is L = 7 + 1), *The System* moves the *Pointer* to the next byte of the data. To avoid *Misalignment,* it restores the initial values of both *Margins.*

Practice:

- Start the T2 tool with the *Background Graphic* of 131x80 pixels.
- Use the **[6]** key to *Scroll the Window* to the right with the *Smart System.*
- Write down the *Margins* values in the following table.

Scrolling to the Right	Address of Display Pointer (AddrB)	Left Margin (L)	Right Margin (R)
Initial Values			
1 pixel			
2 pixels			
3 pixels			
4 pixels			
5 pixels			
6 pixels			
7 pixels			
8 pixels			
9 pixels			
9 pixels			
10 pixels			
11 pixels			
12 pixels			

Note that when the *Left Margin* is increased to values greater than 3, the *Smart System* reduces the *Right Margin* by 2 nibble to avoid the effect of *Misalignment* on the *Screen.*

Note that when the *Left Margin* value is equal to 7, and we press the **[6]** key once more to *Scroll the Window* one pixel further to the right, the *Smart System* increases the *Pointer* value. (AddrB) and restores the *Left Margin* and *Right Margin* to their *Initial Values.*

If we continue *Scrolling the Window* to the right, the *Smart System* will repeat the same process.

Notice how the *Right Margin* values alternate.

You can use the **[4]** key to *Scroll the Window* in the opposite direction using the *Smart System*.

Hardware
Display Panels.

Front Panel or Columns Panel.

The following images show part of the *Front Panel* of the HP48's *Display*. We can see the lines to connect the *Elastomeric Connector,* they join the *Display* to the lines on the HP-48 *Motherboard*. Some of these lines go to the CPU and others to the *Columns Drivers Chips.* The HP-48 has two of the latter.

Although the lines drawn on the panel can conduct electricity, it is covered with a transparent insulating material, so that the *Liquid Crystal* receives the effects of the electric field, but without any current flowing through it.

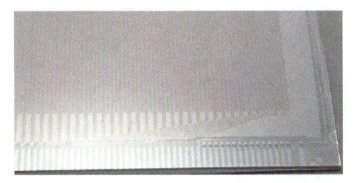 

Rare Panel or Rows Panel.

The *Rare Panel* receives signals from the *Front Panel* through a series of jumpers located in the corners of both *Panels.*

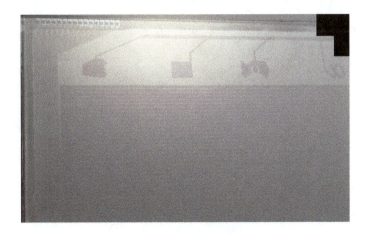

CHAPTER 6
THE SPRITES

6.1 What is a Sprite?

We will use the word *Sprite* to refer to a fixed-size *Graphic Object* that can be drawn on top of another larger *Graphic Object* to enrich it, giving visual presence to elements with which the user interacts in some way. An example of a *Sprite* is the cursor graphic in the PICT environment.

In a game, characters can be represented on the *Screen* using *Sprites,* These usually move in different directions, and interact with other elements of the game. To graphically represent dynamic components of a program, a series of *Sprites can be used* that alternate according to the changes experienced by the component they represent.

In a simulator, a graphic can be placed in one of the *Screen Grobs* to represent the visual environment, and then *Sprites* can be drawn to represent the different components involved in the simulation. As the simulated elements interact, they can move horizontally and vertically, and undergo alterations that can also be represented graphically.

6.2 Sprite Drawing Modes

There are different ways to draw a *Sprite* to the *Screen:*
1) Overwriting the destination area.
2) Logically combining with the destination area.
   a. In AND mode*Pointer* s
   b. In OR mode
   c. In XOR mode

In *Overwrite Mode,* each pixel of the *Background Graphic* is replaced by the corresponding pixel of the *Sprite.*

In *Logical Mode,* each pixel of the *Background Graphic* will be combined with the corresponding pixel of the *Sprite,* using one of the boolean logical operations: AND, OR, XOR

In this chapter we will see different techniques and examples on how to use *Sprites* in our programs.

6.3 Sprite Data Reading Techniques.

The first step to use a *Sprite* is to read its data. For this we can use two techniques:
- Read data from the stack.
- Place the *Sprite* data in the code.

6.4 Reading data from the stack

To read data from a *Graphic Object* that is located in Level 1 of the stack, we can use the *Stack Pointer* D1.

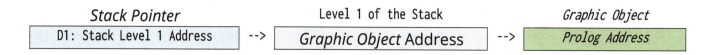

You must apply indirection until you reach the *Graphic Object*. We can do, for example:
```
C=DAT1 A
D1=C
```

Note: we could also use *Register* A:
```
A=DAT1 A
D1=A
```

After this, *Register* D1 will point to the first nibble of the *Graphic Object,* that is, to its *Prolog*:

	Prolog	Size	N Rows	N Columns	Bitmap
D1-->	+5-->	+10-->	+15-->	+20-->	

To read the data from the *Bitmap* we must then increase D1 by 20, since the *Prolog*, the *Size*, the *Number of Rows* and the *Number of Columns* are encoded with 5 nibbles each, giving a total of 20 nibbles. Therefore, to reach the *Bitmap* we can do:
```
D1+16
D1+4                    % 16+4= 20
```

Note: We could also write:
```
D1+10
D1+10                   % 10+10= 20
```

or any other sum that totals 20.

Now D1 points to *Bitmap* of the *Graphic Object,* and we can read its data to use as we want.

	Prolog	Size	N Rows	N Columns	Bitmap

D1-->

6.5 Embedding Sprites's Bitmaps Directly in Code.

As we know, during a *Subroutine* call, *The System* automatically saves the address of the next *Instruction* in the *Return Stack* (RSTK), so that in case of returning from the *Subroutine* the flow of execution can continue at that point. We will take advantage of this feature to embed the *Bitmap* of our *Sprite* in the code itself.

What we do is basically place our *Sprite* after a jump to a *Subroutine* within our code, thus getting its address to be saved in the *Return Stack*. Then we read the address of the *Sprite* in the C *Register,* doing:

    C=RSTK

Let's see an example.

Example: Write code to retrieve data from the next *Sprite,* embedded in the code itself.

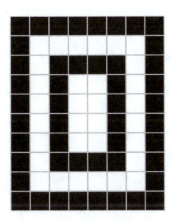

It's *System RPL* encoding is:

    GROB 0001EA000080000FF18DB5A5A5A5ADB18FF

Its *Internal Encoding* in ASM is:

    E1B2032000A000080000FF18DB5A5A5A5ADB18FF

101

We will use this last one:

```
CODE
SAVE
GOSUB Start
$E1B2032000A000080000FF18DB5A5A5A5ADB18FF
*Start
C=RSTK
D1=C
D1+16
D1+4          % Now D1 points to Bitmap of the Sprite.

LOAD
RPL
ENDCODE
@
```

Sometimes we can ignore the *Header*. Then the code will be:

```
CODE
SAVE
GOSUB Start
$FF18DB5A5A5A5ADB18FF
*Start
C=RSTK
D1=C          % Now D1 points to Bitmap of the Sprite.

LOAD
RPL
ENDCODE
@
```

We can easily obtain the *Internal Encoding* of a grob by placing it on the stack and executing the →**H** command, which is part of **Library 256** of the HP49G/49G+/50G.

If we are interested in obtaining It's *System RPL* encoding, we just need to place the grob on the stack and execute **RPLED** from the *Library* **EMacs.**

102

6.6 Sprites on Stack Grob.

In the following example, we will take the *Sprite* from level 1 of the stack and draw it into the *Stack Grob*. The *Sprite* will be a 8x10 pixel *Graphic Object*. We will proceed by reading the *Sprite* one *Row* at a time, and writing the data from the read *Row* into the defined position in the *Stack Grob*.

```
        CODE
        SAVE

        A=DAT1 A
        D1=A



        D1+10
        D1+10       % Now D1 points to Bitmap of the Sprite.

        D0=806D5    % D0->ADISP.
        C=DAT0 A    % C = Stack Grob address.
        D0=C        % D0-> Stack Grob.
        D0+10
        D0+10       % D0-> Stack Grob Bitmap.

        LA 09       % 10 Rows minus one, for the next
                    % loop counter.

        *SetRow
        C=DAT1 B    % Read a Row from the Sprite, that is
                    % 2 nibbles = 8 pixels.
        DAT0=C B    % Write data to Stack Grob.

        D1+2        % Point to the next Row of the Sprite.
        D0+34       % Point to the next Row of the Stack Grob.

        A-1 B       % Decrement Rows counter.
        GONC SetRow    % If not the last Row, repeat the loop.

        LOAD
        RPL
        ENDCODE
        @
```

In order to observe the effects of the aforementioned code, it is necessary to freeze the screen following its execution. For the present purposes, we will employ a straightforward technique to accomplish this:

```
<< Sprite Code 0 WAIT DROP >>
```

or:

```
::
        Sprite ID
        ID Code
        %0
        WaitForKey
        2DROP
    ;
    @
```

As you can see, the code in the previous example always places the *Sprite* in the top left of the *Stack Grob*. We can rewrite the code to place it in other areas of the Screen *by* applying the simple ideas we will see in the next section.

6.7 Columns of Nibble.

As we know, each *Row* of the *Stack Grob* has 34 nibbles, so instead of *Columns* of pixels, we can imagine the *Screen* being made up of *Columns of Nibble*.

Below is an image to illustrate this idea. We have a grid that represents the HP50G *Stack Grob*, with its 72 *Rows* of 34 nibbles each.

The term *Column of Nibble* refers to each of these stripes.

In the last example of the previous section, a *Sprite* was successfully drawn into the *Stack Grob,* Since the insertion was started with D0 pointing to the start of the *Bitmap,* the *Sprite* ended up in the top left corner of the *Screen*, as shown below:

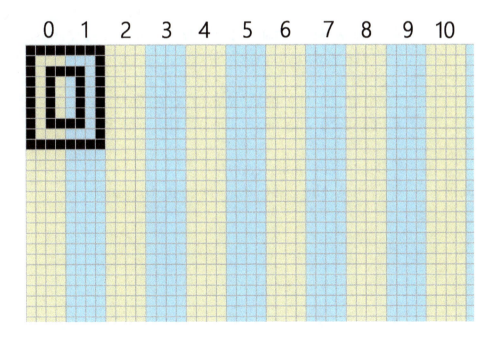

Simply start loading the *Sprite* with D0 pointing to another *Column of Nibble* so that the *Sprite* will be displayed in that area. Let's see an example:

Let's rewrite the code on the previous example to display the *Sprite* in the third *Column of Nibble* of the *Stack Grob:*

```
CODE
SAVE


A=DAT1 A
D1=A
D1+10
D1+10               % Now D1 point to Bitmap of the Sprite.

D0=806D5            % D0->ADISP
C=DAT0 A            % C =        Stack Grob address.
D0=C                % D0-> Stack Grob.
D0+10
D0+10               % D0-> Stack Grob Bitmap.
D0+2                % Increment D0 to display the Sprite in the third column.

LA 09               % 10 Rows minus one, for the next loop counter


*SetRow
C=DAT1 B            % Read a Row from the Sprite, that is 2 nibbles = 8 pixels.
DAT0=C B            % Write data to Stack Grob.

D1+2                % Point to the next Row of the Sprite.
D0+34               % Point to the next Row of the Stack Grob.

A-1 B               % Decrement Rows counter.
GONC SetRow         % If not the last Row, repeat the loop.

LOAD
RPL
ENDCODE
@
```

Note:

The portion of code that have been modified are marked in red.

In this code, instead of starting the loading of the *Sprite* with D0 pointing to the start of the Stack *Grob Bitmap*, the loading has been started two nibbles later. This has been achieved with the *Instruction* D0+2, In the following image we can see the result.

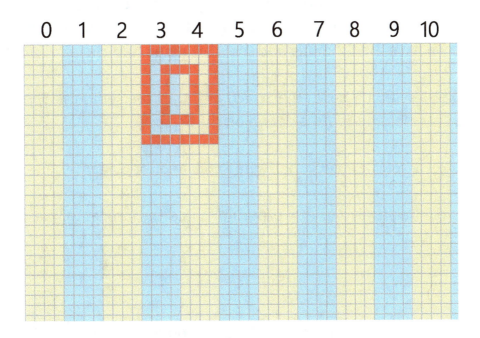

If we want to place the *Sprite* in any *Column of Nibble* **n**, we would only have to replace the **2** in the previous code with the desired value **n.**

Exercise:
> a) Rewrite the above code so that the *Sprite* is displayed in the seventh *Column of Nibble* of the *Grob Stack.*
> b) Rewrite the program by placing the *Sprite* as part of the code, using C=RSTK to read its address.
> c) Rewrite the above code to display the *Sprite* in the *PICT Grob* instead of the *Stack Grob.*
> d) Rewrite to display the *Sprite* in the *PICT Grob* taking into account the *Right Margin* when writing the Columns.

6.8 Using other Sprites insertion modes.

In the previous example we put the *Sprite* in overwrite mode. That is, the data in the *Stack Grob* was replaced by the data in the *Sprite.* Sometimes the programmer does not want to overwrite the data, but wants the data in the *Screen* to affect the data to be placed. Among these new modes we have the OR mode and the AND mode.

In OR mode, a pixel is set if it is set in the *Screen* or if they are set in the *Sprite.* In either case the pixel must be set when the *Sprite* is drawn on the *Screen.*

In AND mode, a pixel is set if it is set in both the *Sprite* and the *Screen.*

These operations are relatively easy to program, since the processor has *Instructions* that carry them out.

Let's see an example:

Example: Rewrite the example from the previous section to place the data in OR mode.

```
        CODE
        SAVE

        A=DAT1 A
        D1=A
        D1+10
        D1+10           % Now D1 point to Bitmap of the Sprite.

        D0=806D5        % D0->ADISP
        C=DAT0 A        % C = Stack Grob address.
        D0=C            % D0-> Stack Grob.
        D0+10
        D0+10           % D0-> Stack Grob Bitmap.
        D0+2            % Increment D0 to display the Sprite in the third column.

        LC 09           % 10 Rows minus one, for the next loop counter.
        B=C B

        *SetRow
        C=DAT1 B        % Read a Row from the Sprite, that is 2 nibbles = 8 pixels.
        A=DAT0 B
```

```
C=C!A  B
DAT0=C  B              % Write data to Stack Grob.

D1+2                   % Point to the next Row of the Sprite.
D0+34                  % Point to the next Row of the Stack Grob.

B-1  B                 % Decrement Rows counter.
GONC SetRow            % If not the last Row, repeat the loop.

LOAD
RPL
ENDCODE
@
```

We modified the code to use *Register* B as the *Rows Counter* instead of *Register* A.

Instead of just placing the *Sprite* data, it is now processed taking into account the *Screen* data, by running:
```
A=DAT0  B
C=C!A  B
```

Exercise: Rewrite the previous example so that:
  a) The data is placed in XOR mode.
  b) Use a 12x10 pixel *Sprite*.

6.9 Copying Screen Areas.

Before drawing a *Sprite* to the *Screen,* it's common to save a copy of the area where it will be placed, so that we can restore that area when removing the *Sprite.* By "restore" we mean making it look like it was before the *Sprite* was placed.

To move a *Sprite* on the *Screen,* the following steps are usually followed:
  1) Restore the area where the *Sprite* is located
  2) Save a copy of the new area where the *Sprite* will be placed.
  3) Place the *Sprite* in the new location.

The preceding section illustrated *Sprite* insertion onto the *Screen*. This section details the procedure for saving a copy of the *Screen* area prior to *Sprite* placement. The steps outlined below will be followed:

1) Create a grob of the same dimensions as the *Sprite,* using the makegrob *Subroutine*.

2) Read the data from the area where the *Sprite* will be placed and write it on the new grob created in the previous step.

The makegrob *Subroutine* creates a grob of size W x H, given W in R0.A, H in R1.A. the CPU *Register* D0 will point to the body of the grob, whose *Prolog* is located at D0-20.

Example: Write a code to generates a copy of an 8 x 10 pixel region of the *Screen*, in the first two *Columns of Nibble* of the *Stack Grob.*

```
CODE
SAVE

LC 00008
R0=C A              % W
LC 0000A            % Ah = 10d
R1=C A              % H

GOSBVL makegrob     % D0-> Bitmap of the new grob.
CD0EX
D0=C
R2=C A              % Save Bitmap address of new grob in R2.
D0=806D5            % D0->ADISP.
C=DAT0 A            % C = Stack Grob address.
D0=C                % D0-> Stack Grob.
D0+10
D0+10               % D0-> Stack Grob Bitmap.

A=R1 A
A-1 A               % H Rows minus one, for the next loop counter.

*CopyRow
C=DAT1 B            % Read 2 nibbles (8 pixels) from Stack Grob.
DAT0=C B            % Write data to new grob.
```

110

```
D1+34              % Point to the next Row of the Stack Grob.
D0+2               % Point to the next Row of the new grob.

A-1 B              % Decreasing Rows counter.
GONC CopyRow       % If not the last Row, repeat the loop.

LOAD

D-1 A
D1-5
LA 00014
C=R2 A             % Address of new grob bitmap.
C=C-A A            % Subtract 20d to obtain the address of the Prolog.
DAT1=C A           % The Stack Pointer now has the address of the new grob.

RPL
ENDCODE
@
```

Exercise:
   a) Write code to generates a copy of an 8 x 20 pixel region of the *Screen*, in the first two *Columns of Nibble* of the *Stack Grob*.
   b) Rewrite your code to copy the data from the *Stack Grob* starting on the third *Column*.

Example: Rewrite the code from the previous example to extract the data from the third *Column of Nibble* of the *Stack Grob,* and make the copied area 12d x 24d pixels.

```
CODE
SAVE

LC 0000C           % Ch = 12d.
R0=C A             % W

LC 00018           % 18h = 24d.
R1=C A             % H
```

```
GOSBVL makegrob   % D0-> Bitmap of the new grob.
CD0EX
D0=C
R2=C A            % Save Bitmap address of new grob in R2.


D0=806D5          % D0->ADISP.
C=DAT0 A          % C = Stack Grob address.
D0=C              % D0-> Stack Grob.
D0+10
D0+10             % D0-> Stack Grob Bitmap
D1+2              % Increasing the Pointer to the third Column of Nibble.
                  % First column D1+0; Second D1+1; Third D1+2.


A=R1 A
A-1 A             % H Rows minus one, for the next loop counter.


*CopyRow
C=DAT1 X          % Read 3 nibbles (12 pixels) from the Stack Grob.
DAT0=C X          % Write data to new grob.


D1+34             % Point to the next Row of the Stack Grob.
D0+ 4             % Point to the next Row of the new grob.


A-1 B             % Decreasing Rows counter.
GONC CopyRow      % If not the last Row, repeat the loop.


LOAD


D-1 A
D1-5
LA 00014
C=R2 A            % Address of new grob bitmap.
C=C-A A           % Subtract 20d to obtain the address of the Prolog.
DAT1=C A          % The Stack Pointer now has the address of the new grob.


RPL
ENDCODE
@
```

Note that, although 3 nibbles are copied from each *Row,* to advance the *Pointer* D0 to the next *Row* of the *Sprite* we need to add 4. This is because the *Rows* of any grob always have an even number of nibbles.

Exercise: Rewrite the code on the previous example to extract the data from the seventh *Column of Nibble* of the *Stack Grob.* The copied area has to be 16d x 8d pixels.

Example: Rewrite the code in the previous example to extract the data from the eighth *Row* of the *Screen.*

In this case we must start the reading sequence by pointing seven *rows* down. The increment needed for this will be:

      7x34d =238d

We can take advantage of this to include here the 20 nibbles of the jump from the *Prolog* to the *Stack Grob Bitmap:*

      (7x34d) + 20 =258d

Let's also add the increment of 2 nibbles needed for the jump to the third *Column*:
(7x34d) + 20 + 2 =260d =104h

So the new code will be:

```
CODE
SAVE

LC 0000C              % Ch = 12d
R0=C A                % W
LC 00018              % 18h = 24d
R1=C A                % H

GOSBVL makegrob       % D0-> Bitmap of the new grob.
CD0EX
D0=C
R2=C A                % Save Bitmap address of new grob in R2.
```

```
D1=806D5          % D1->ADISP
C=DAT1 A          % C= address of the Stack Grob Bitmap.
LA 00104
C=C+A A
D1=C

A=R1 A
A-1 A             % H Rows minus one, for the next loop counter.

*CopyRow
C=DAT1 X          % Read 3 nibbles (12 pixels) from Stack Grob.
DAT0=C X          % Write data to new grob.

D1+34             % Point to the next Row of the Stack Grob.
D0+4              % Point to the next Row of the new grob.

A-1 B             % Decreasing Rows counter.
GONC CopyRow      % If not the last Row, repeat the loop.

LOAD

D-1 A
D1-5
LA 00014
C=R2 A            % Bitmap address of new grob.
C=C-A A           % Subtract 20d to obtain the address of the Prolog.
DAT1=C A          % The Stack Pointer now has the address of the new grob.

RPL
ENDCODE
@
```

Exercise: Rewrite the code from the previous example to extract the data from *Row* 32 of the *Screen*.

6.10 Coordenates and Screen Areas.

We can imagine the screen divided into 34 *Columns* and 80 *Rows* (64 *Rows* on the HP49G). The *Rows* are given in pixels, while the columns are groups of four pixels (nibbles). We can establish a coordinate system, similar to the one used by default in *System RPL*, where the origin of the system will be in the upper left corner of the screen (coordinates 0,0), and the values increase downwards and to the right.

This coordinate system enables the unambiguous identification of *Screen* locations through *Row* and *Column of Nibble* designations.

A system like this offers many advantages to the programmer, such as easy access and management of *Screen* data, since the *HP Saturn CPU* has *Instructions* for easy and fast access to the nibbles through the D0 and D1 *Pointers*. To point to the next nibble, simply increment these *Pointers* using D0+n and D1+n. To point to a specific area, simply load its address into *Registers* A or C and execute one of the *Instructions*: D0=A.A, D0=C.A, D1=A.A or D1=C.A.

If we point D0 or D1 to any nibble in the *Bitmap* displayed on the *Screen,* it is easy to switch to the nibble just below it by incrementing the *Pointer* by a number equal to the *Rows Size* (in nibbles). Remember that the *Rows Size* will be equal to 34 in the *Stack Grob,* but equal to 34+RM in the *PICT Grob.* Therefore, to point to the nibble just below the current one, just run:

when we are working on the *Stack Grob:*

        D0+34
or:
        D1+34

when we are working on the *PICT Grob:*

        D0+34 +RM
or:
        D1+34 +RM

Example: Write a code that, given the x,y coordinates of a region of the *Stack Grob,* returns an 8x12 pixel copy of its contents. The x coordinate is given in terms of *Columns of Nibble.* The resulting grob is returned at level 1 of the stack.

CODE
% This code requires two binary integers #x, #y on the stack indicating
% the coordinates of a region of the *Stack Grob.*
% The #x coordinate is taken from level 2 of the stack, and #y from level 1.
% The grob generated by the code is 8x12 pixels.

SAVE

```
GOSBVL POP2#          % 2: x ->A.A 1: y ->C.A
R2=C A                % R2= y
R4=A A                % R4= x


LC 00008
R0=C A                % W
LC 0000C
R1=C A                % H
GOSBVL makegrob


CD0EX
R1=C A                % R1= BODY ADDR.
D1=C                  % D1->BODY.


C=R2 A
B=C A                 % B= y


LC 00022              % Nibbles in a Row of the Stack Grob: 34d=22h.
A=0 A


*Mult                 % Calculating at how many nibbles from the origin
                      % of the Coordinate System the Row and the Stack Grob
                      % are found.
B-1 A                 % Add 34d, y-1 times.
GOC Cont
A=A+C A
GONC Mult


*Cont
R3=A A                % Save the result in R3.


LC 0000C              % Number of Rows to copy.
C-1 A                 % Adjusting for exit when Overflow.
```

```
B=C A                 % Initializing Rows counter.

D0=806D5              % D0->ADISP
A=DAT0 A              % A = @StackGrob

LC 00014              % 14h= 20d
A=A+C A               % Skip the Header.
                      % A=@StackGrob +20d

C=R4 A                % C= x = Horizontal jump (HJ).
A=A+C A               % A= @StackGrob + 20d + x

C=R3 A                % C= 34(y-1) = Vertical Jump (VJ).
A=A+C A               % A= @StackGrob + 20d + x + 34(y-1).

D0=A                  % D0 point to nibble in Row y-1, Column of Nibble x
                      % of the Stack Grob.

*LoadBMap             % Read data from the Stack Grob, Row by Row,
                      % and write it to the new grob.
C=DAT0 B
DAT1=C B

D0+34                 % Next Row of Stack Grob.
D1+2                  % Next Row of the new grob.
B=B-1 A               % Decrement the counter.
GONC LoadBMap

LOAD
D1+5
D+1 A

C=R1 A
C=C-10 A
C=C-10 A
DAT1=C A

RPL
ENDCODE
@
```

Example: Rewrite the above code so that the extracted area is 4 x 7 pixels. This is the size of a small font on the calculator *Screen*.

```
CODE
% This code requires two binary integers #x, #y on the stack indicating
% the coordinates of a Stack Grob region. The #x coordinate is taken from
% level 2 of the stack, and #y from level 1. The grob generated by the
% code is 4x8 pixels.

SAVE

GOSBVL POP2#        % 2: x ->A.A 1: y ->C.A
R2=C A              % R2= y
R4=A A              % R4= x


LC 00004
R0=C A              % W
LC 00007
R1=C A              % H
GOSBVL makegrob


CD0EX
R1=C A              % R1= BODY ADDR
D1=C                % D1->BODY
C=R2 A
B=C A               % B= y


LC 00022            % Nibbles in a Row of the Stack Grob: 34d=22h.
A=0 A


*Mult               % Calculating at how many nibbles from the origin
                    % of the Coordinate System the Row and the Stack Grob
                    % are found.


B-1 A               % Add 34d, y-1 times.
GOC Cont
A=A+C A
GONC Mult


*Cont
R3=A A              % Save the result in R3.
```

```
LC 00007          % Number of Rows to Copy.
C-1 A             % Adjusting for exit when Overflow.
B=C A             % Initializing Rows counter.

D0=806D5          % D0->ADISP
A=DAT0 A          % A = @StackGrob.

LC 00014          % 14h= 20d
A=A+C A           % Skip the Header.
                  % A=@StackGrob +20d.

C=R4 A            % C= x = Horizontal jump (HJ).
A=A+C A           % A= @StackGrob + 20d + x

C=R3 A            % C= 34(y-1) = Vertical Jump (VJ).
A=A+C A           % A= @StackGrob + 20d + x + 34(y-1).

D0=A              % D0 point to nibble in Row y-1, Column of Nibble x
                  % of the Stack Grob.

*LoadBMap         % Read data from the Stack Grob, Row by Row,
                  % and write it to the new grob.
C=DAT0 1
DAT1=C 1

D0+34             % Next Row of Stack Grob.
D1+2              % Next Row of new grob.
                  % The number of nibbles in a Row is always an even integer.
B=B-1 A           % Decrement counter.
GONC LoadBMap

LOAD
D1+5
D+1 A

C=R1 A
C=C-10 A
C=C-10 A
DAT1=C A
```

```
RPL
ENDCODE
@
```

Exercise:

a) Rewrite the code in the previous example so that the extracted area is 12 x 14 pixels.

b) Rewrite the code to work on the *PICT Grob,* when RM = 0.

c) Rewrite the code to work on the *PICT Grob,* when RM >0.

6.11 Drawing Sprites on specific Screen Area.

We will approach this topic in a similar way as we did in the previous section, with a *Coordinate System* based on *Columns of Nibble.* We will use the POP2# *Instruction* to read the coordinates given on the stack, and we will use the D0 and D1 *Registers* to point to the *Graphic Object* and *Stack Grob Bitmaps.*

Example: Write a code in *HP Saturn Assembly Language* which, given an 8x12 grob and two coordinates #x, #y, on the stack, places the grob at the specified coordinates of the *Stack Grob.* The coordinates are binary integers. The x coordinate is given in *Columns of Nibble.*

```
CODE
% This code requires a grob and two binary integers #x, #y on the stack.
% These last ones indicate the coordinates of a region of the
% Stack Grob where you want to place the grob.
% The #x coordinate is taken from level 2 of the stack, the #y coordinate
% is taken from level 1.
% The grob, given at level 3 of the stack, must be 8 x 12 pixels.

SAVE
```

```
GOSBVL POP2#      % 2: x ->A A       1: y ->C.A
R2=C A            % R2= y
R4=A A            % R4= x
                  % The POP2# instruction updated the RPL Pointers,
                  % and now D1->given grob.


B=C A             % B= y

LC 00022          % Nibbles in a Row of the Stack Grob: 34d=22h.
A=0 A             % Cleaning A.A.

*Mult             % Calculating at how many nibbles from the origin
                  % of the Coordinate System the Row and the Stack Grob
                  % are found.
B-1 A             % Add 34d, y-1 times.
GOC Cont
A=A+C A
GONC Mult

*Cont
R3=A A            % Save the result in R3.

LC 0000C          % Height of the given grob, which is equal to the
                  % number of Rows to copy into Stack Grob (12d= Ch).
C-1 A             % Adjusting for counting based on Overflow.
B=C A             % Initializing Rows counter.

C=DAT1 A          % Address of the given grob.
D1=C              % D1->given grob.
D1+10             % Skip the Header.
D1+10             % D1-> Bitmap of the given grob.

D0=806D5          % D0->ADISP
A=DAT0 A          % A = @StackGrob

LC 00014          % 14h= 20d
A=A+C A           % Skip the Header.
                  % A=@StackGrob +20d.

C=R4 A            % C= x = Horizontal jump (HJ).
```

```
A=A+C  A            % A= @StackGrob + 20d + x

C=R3  A             % C= 34(y-1) = Vertical Jump (VJ)
A=A+C  A            % A= @StackGrob + 20d + x + 34(y-1).

D0=A                % D0 point to nibble in Row y-1, Column of Nibble x of
                    % the Stack Grob.

*LoadBMap           % Read data from the Stack Grob, Row by Row, and
                    % write it to the new grob.
C=DAT1  B           % B=2
DAT0=C  B
D0+34               % Next Row of Stack Grob.
D1+2                % Next Row of new grob.
                    % The number of nibbles in a Row is always an even integer.
B=B-1  A            % Decrement the Counter.
GONC  LoadBMap

LOAD
D1+15
D+3  A

RPL
ENDCODE
@
```

Example: Rewrite the code above so that it can use a graphic that is 12 pixels wide and any number of pixels tall.

```
CODE
% This code requires a grob and two binary integers #x, #y on the stack.
% The integers #x, #y indicate the coordinates of a region of
% the Stack Grob where you want to place the grob.
% The #x coordinate is taken from level 2 of the stack, the #y coordinate
% is taken from level 1.
% The grob, given at level 3 of the stack, must be 8 pixels wide,
% but the height has no restrictions.
% Warning: Be careful not to write outside the Screen memory.

SAVE
```

```
GOSBVL POP2#          % 2: x ->A.A 1: y ->C.A
R2=C A                % R2= y
R4=A A                % R4= x
                      % The POP2# Instruction updated the RPL Pointers,
                      % and now D1->given grob.


B=C A                 % B= y

LC 00022              % Nibbles in a Row of the Stack Grob: 34d=22h
A=0 A                 % Cleaning A.A

*Mult                 % Calculating at how many nibbles from the origin
                      % of the Coordinate System the Row and the Stack Grob
                      % are found.

B-1 A                 % Add 34d, y-1 times.
GOC Cont
A=A+C A
GONC Mult

*Cont
R3=A A                % Save the result in R3.

C=DAT1 A              % Address of the given grob.
D1=C                  % D1->given grob.
D1+10                 % Skip the Prolog and Size.
C=DAT1 A              % C= Number of Columns of the given grob.
C-1 A                 % Adjusting for counting based on Overflow.
B=C A                 % Initializing Rows counter of given grob.
D1+10                 % D1-> Bitmap of the given grob.

D0=806D5              % D0->ADISP.
A=DAT0 A              % A = @StackGrob.

LC 00014              %14h= 20d
A=A+C A               % Skip the Header.
                      % A=@StackGrob +20d.

C=R4 A                % C= x = Horizontal jump (HJ).
A=A+C A               % A= @StackGrob + 20d + x
```

```
C=R3  A              % C= 34(y-1) = Vertical Jump (VJ).
A=A+C  A             % A= @StackGrob + 20d + x + 34(y-1).


D0=A                 % D0 point to nibble in Row y-1, Column of Nibble x of
                     % the Stack Grob.


*LoadBMap            % Read data from the Stack Grob, Row by Row, and write
                     % it to the new grob.
C=DAT1  X            % X= 3nibbles = 12 pixels.
DAT0=C  X
D0+34                % Next Row of Stack Grob.
D1+ 4                % Next Row of new grob.
                     % The number of nibbles in a Row is always an even integer.
B=B-1  A             % Decrement the Counter.
GONC  LoadBMap


LOAD
D1+15
D+3  A
RPL
ENDCODE
@
```

Note that in the LoadBMap *Subroutine*, even though the given grob is 12 pixels wide, i.e. 3 nibbles, it is necessary to add 4 to D1 to jump to the next *Row* (D1+4). This is because, as the *Width* of every grob is always an even number of nibbles, the given grob is internally encoded 4 nibbles wide. It is important to keep this in mind when working with *Graphic Objects*,

---

Exercise:
   a) Rewrite the code in the previous example to prevent it from writing to *Memory Spaces* that are outside of graphics memory.
   b) Rewrite the code in the previous example so that it works on the *PICT Grob* instead of the *Stack Grob,* taking into account the value of the *Right Margin*.

Hardware
Perimeter seal and Panels interconnection.

Conduction lines between panels.

Although the Display has two glass *Panels*, only one of them, the *Front Panel,* is in direct contact with the *Elastomeric Connectors.* Signals sent to the *Rare Panel* are transmitted through conductors that go from the *Front Panel* to the *Rare Panel.*

These conductors appear as circles in the following images:

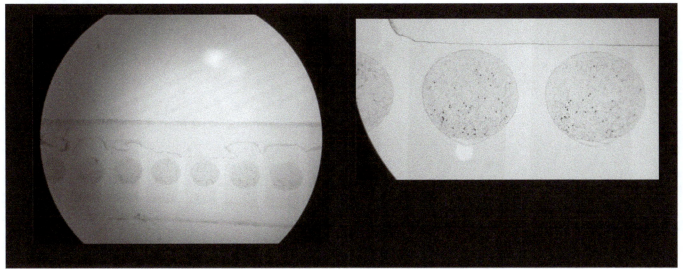

Conductors that transmit signals from the *Front Panel* to the *Rare Panel,*
In the image on the right we see them closer.

The perimeter seal

In this image we can see part of the perimeter seal of one of the *Panels.* The function of this substance is to prevent the *Liquid Crystal* from leaking out of the space between the two *Panels.* In addition, it keeps the *Panels* adhered to each other by their edges:

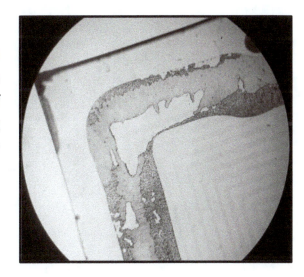

125

CHAPTER 7
WORKING AT THE BITS LEVEL

7.1 Working at the bits level.

In the previous chapter we learned how to draw graphics on the *Screen* in specific areas defined at nibbles level. This is relatively easy since the increments in *Registers* D0 and D1 also work at nibble level, and the CPU has *Instructions* to jump from one nibble to another.

To work on intermediate positions, i.e. starting from a specific bit within the nibble, we need more elaborate codes. It's going to be necessary to read the *Sprite* data, shift its bits to the desired position and place the "modified *Sprite*" on top of the *Screen* data. This brings up a new problem: how to write over the *Screen* data starting from a specific bit, without overwriting the other bits that are part of the nibble? In this section we will see techniques to effectively handle these interesting situations.

7.2 Logical operations with Registers

The *HP Saturn CPU* allows logical operations to be performed on data in the *Registers.*

Logical Operations	Symbols	Example
AND	&	A=A&C X C=C&A A
OR	!	A=A!C B C=C!D W
XOR	^	C=C^A A

7.3 Unset specific pixels

We can use logical operations to disable specific pixels.

Example: *Register* D0 points to a specific nibble of the grob on the *Screen:*

```
...
C=DAT0 X    % Read three nibbles of data in C.
LA FF0      % Load a mask in A. FF0h = 1111 1111 0000.
C=C&A X     % The bits in the first nibble are set to zero.
```

```
DAT0=C X    % Pixels are unset.
...
```

Remember that the bits appearing on the right in *Registers* A or C correspond to the pixels displayed on the left on the *Screen.*

What if we only want to disable the first two pixels? To do this we just need to modify the mask.

Let's see an example:

Example: Rewrite the above code to disable only the first two pixels:

```
...
C=DAT0 X        % Read three nibbles of data in C:
LA FFC          % Mask: FFCh= 1111 1111 1100.
C=C&A X         % The first two bits in the first nibble are set to zero.
DAT0=C X        % Pixels are unset.
...
```

Let's write some code to disable alternating pixels from the data.

Example: Rewrite the above code to disable alternating pixels:

```
...
C=DAT0 X        % Read three nibbles of data in C:
LA AAA          % Mask: AAAh= 1010 1010 1010.
C=C&A X         % Bits are set to zero in alternating positions.
DAT0=C X        % Pixels are unset.
...
```

Exercise: Rewrite the previous examples to use *Register* D1 instead of D0. Also, instead of reading three nibbles of data (X), 2 nibbles (B) should be read.

7.4 Set specific pixels.

What if instead of unset, we want to set the pixels alternately? In this case we will use the logical operation OR. Let's see an example:

Example: Write a code to alternately set the pixels read from the *Screen*. The D0 CPU *Register* points to the data of interest:

```
...
C=DAT0 X    % Read three nibbles of data in C:
LA 555      % Mask: 555h= 0101 0101 0101.
C=C!A  X    % Bits are zeroed in alternating positions.
DAT0=C X    % Pixels are unset.
...
```

Note that in this example, the bits where the mask has a value of zero will hold the value of the original data:

```
1 OR 0 = 1
0 OR 0 = 0
```

while the bits where the mask has a value of 1 will be set to 1, regardless of their previous value:

```
1 OR 1 = 1
0 OR 1 = 1
```

Exercise:
  a) Rewrite the previous code to set the last six pixels read, keeping the rest unchanged.
  b) Rewrite the above code to set the first and last pixel read, keeping the rest unchanged. Also, the reading should be five nibbles instead of three.

7.5 Bits Level Shifting

We often want the *Sprite* drawn on the *Screen* to move smoothly. Nibble jumps may be too abrupt, and we may prefer a transition of less than a nibble at a time. In this case, we need to perform "bit-level shifts" on the read data.

We know that to draw a grob to the *Screen,* we do it *Row* by *Row,* We must read the data, shift it, and then draw it at the desired position.

To the left:

Shifting the data in a *Register* to the left has the same effect as multiplying by two. We can achieve this by adding the *Register* to itself:

```
...
LC FEFFF    % C= ... 1111 1110 1111 1111 1111
C=C+C A     % C= ... 1111 1101 1111 1111 1110
C=C+C A     % C= ... 1111 1011 1111 1111 1100
C=C+C A     % C= ... 1111 0111 1111 1111 1000
C=C+C A     % C= ... 1110 1111 1111 1111 0000
...
```

As we can see, each time we add a *Register* to itself, its bits are shifted one bit to the left.

To the right:

To shift data in a *Register* one bit **to the right,** the *HP Saturn* provides the following *Instructions:*

```
ASRB  Shift to the right the 64 bits of the Register A
BSRB  Shift to the right the 64 bits of the Register B
CSRB  Shift to the right the 64 bits of the Register C
DSRB  Shift to the right the 64 bits of the Register D
```

Let's see an example:

```
...
LC 0FEFFF   % C= ... 1111 1110 1111 1111 1111
CSRB        % C= ... 0111 1111 0111 1111 1111
CSRB        % C= ... 0011 1111 1011 1111 1111
```

```
CSRB        % C= … 0001 1111 1101 1111 1111
CSRB        % C= … 0000 1111 1110 1111 1111
…
```

Note that executing these *instructions* causes the least significant bit of the file to be lost.

ARM-based calculators such as the 50G and 49G+ have some new bit-shifting *instructions* that are not available on the HP48 and 49G. For details, see the MASD manual (p. 6-24).

7.6 Moving a Sprite at the Pixel Level

Let's analyze the following situation:

We have the *Register* **D1** pointing to the *Bitmap* of a *Sprite* whose *Rows* are **n** nibbles each. **D0** point to *Bitmap* of the *Screen*. We want to place the *Sprite* at nibble **k** of the *Screen*. So we'll run a loop that does:

```
…
*LoopX
D0+k        % Increment the Pointer until it points to the nibble
            % to place the Sprite.
C=DAT1 f    % Read a Row from the Sprite, f >= n.
DAT0=C f    % Write the Row data to the Screen memory.

D0+delta    % Increment D0 until it points to the next Row of the Sprite.
D1+gamma    % Increment D1 until it points to the next Row of the Screen.
B-1 B       % Decrement Rows Counter.
GONC LoopX
…
```

The above method always places the *Sprite* at the start of nibble k, meaning it always writes data starting from the first bit of the nibble.

We can enhance the previous code to position the *Sprite* at a specific bit within the nibble. To accomplish this, we'll use a technique combining **bit shifting** and **logical *Register* operations,** two topics covered earlier in this chapter.

What we have to do is:

1) Make a copy, into a *Register,* of the *Screen Area* where we want to place the *Sprite.*
2) Clear the bits that will be occupied by the *Sprite* (using AND).
3) Copy the *Sprite* data into a *Register.*
4) Shift the *Sprite* data to the left (by adding the *Register* to itself).
5) Draw the shifted *Sprite* on the copy of the *Screen Area* (using OR).
6) Draw the resulting graphic to the *Screen.*

This process will be carried out *Row* by *Row,* using a loop, as we did in previous cases.

The copied area of the *Screen* will always be larger than the *Sprite* to be placed. This is important because when we move the *Sprite* bits there will be an increase in the data to be copied.

With this method we will be able to place the *Sprite* over the data that is already on the *Screen,* without overwriting the bits that are not needed, resulting in a very clean insertion of the *Sprite* into the *Screen.*

Keep in mind that data is always inverted when transferred from memory to the *HP Saturn Registers.* This means that a *Left Shift* of data in the *Registers* results in a *Right Shift* on the *Screen,* and vice versa.

Example: Write code to draw a given **8** x **N** *Sprite* to the *Screen.* The *Sprite* should be drawn starting at the second pixel of nibble x.

```
CODE
% This code requires a grob and two binary integers #x, #y on the stack.
% The integers #x, #y indicate the coordinates of a region of the
% Stack Grob where you want to place the grob.
% The #x coordinate is taken from level 2 of the stack,
% the #y coordinate is taken from level 1.
% The grob, given at level 3 of the stack, must be 8 pixels wide
% but the height has no restrictions.
% Warning: Be careful not to write outside the Screen memory.

SAVE
```

```
GOSBVL POP2#          % 2: x ->A.A 1: y ->C.A
R2=C A                % R2= y
R4=A A                % R4= x
                      % Subroutine POP2# updates the RPL Pointers,
                      % and now D1->given grob.


B=C A                 % B= y


LC 00022              % Nibbles in a Row of the Stack Grob: 34d=22h.
A=0 A                 % Cleaning A.A


*Mult                 % Calculating at how many nibbles from the origin
                      % of the Coordinate System the Row and the Stack Grob
                      % are found.


B-1 A                 % Add 34d, y-1 times.
GOC Cont
A=A+C A
GONC Mult


*Cont
R3=A A                % Save the result in R3.


C=DAT1 A              % Address of the given grob.
D1=C                  % D1->given grob.
D1+10                 % Skip the Header.
C=DAT1 A              % C= Number of Rows of the given grob.
C-1 A                 % Adjusting for counting based on Overflow.
B=C A                 % Initializing Rows counter of given grob.
D1+10                 % D1-> Bitmap of the given grob.


D0=806D5              % D0->ADISP.
A=DAT0 A              % A = @StackGrob.
```

```
LC 00014            % 14h= 20d.
A=A+C A             % Skip the Header.
                    % A=@StackGrob +20d


C=R4 A              % C= x = Horizontal jump (HJ).
A=A+C A             % A= @StackGrob + 20d + x


C=R3 A              % C= 34(y-1) = Vertical Jump (VJ).
A=A+C A             % A= @StackGrob + 20d + x + 34(y-1).


D0=A                % D0 point to nibble in Row y-1, Column of Nibble x
                    % of the Stack Grob.

C=0 W
A=0 W


*LoadBMap           % Read data from the Stack Grob, Row by Row, and
                    % write it to a new grob.


LA FFE01            % FFE01h= 1111 1111 1110 0000 0001.
C=DAT0 A
A=A&C A


C=0 A
C=DAT1 B            % B= 2 nibbles = 8 pixels


C=C+C A
C=C!A A


DAT0=C A
D0+34               % Next Row of Stack Grob
D1+2                % Next Row of new grob.
                    % The number of nibbles in a Row is always an even integer.
B=B-1 A             % Decrement the Counter.
GONC LoadBMap



LOAD
D1+15
D+3 A


RPL
```

```
ENDCODE
@
```

Example: Rewrite the previous code to draw a given **8** x **N** *Sprite* onto the *Screen*. The *Sprite* should be placed at the third pixel of nibble x.

```
CODE
% This code requires a grob and two binary integers #x, #y on the stack.
% The integers #x, #y indicate the coordinates of a region of
% the Stack Grob where you want to place the grob.
% The #x coordinate is taken from level 2 of the stack, the #y coordinate
% is taken from level 1.
% The grob, given at level 3 of the stack, must be 8 pixels wide, but the
% height has no restrictions.
% Warning: Be careful not to write outside the Screen memory.

SAVE

GOSBVL POP2#        % 2: x ->A.A 1: y ->C.A
R2=C A              % R2= y
R4=A A              % R4= x
                    % Subroutine POP2# updates the RPL Pointers,
                    % and now D1->given grob.


B=C A               % B= y


LC 00022            % Nibbles in a Row of the Stack Grob: 34d=22h.
A=0 A               % Cleaning A.A.

*Mult               % Calculating at how many nibbles from the origin
                    % of the Coordinate System the Row and the Stack Grob
                    % are found.
B-1 A               % Add 34d, y-1 times.
GOC Cont
A=A+C A
GONC Mult

*Cont
R3=A A              % Save the result in R3.
```

```
C=DAT1 A          % Address of the given grob.
D1=C              % D1->given grob.
D1+10             % Skip the Header.
C=DAT1 A          % C= Number of Rows of the given grob.
C-1 A             % Adjusting for counting based on Overflow.
B=C A             % Initializing Rows counter of given grob.
D1+10             % D1-> Bitmap of the given grob.

D0=806D5          % D0->ADISP
A=DAT0 A          % A = @StackGrob

LC 00014          %14h= 20d
A=A+C A           % Skip the Header.
                  % A=@StackGrob +20d

C=R4 A            % C= x = Horizontal jump (HJ).
A=A+C A           % A= @StackGrob + 20d + x

C=R3 A            % C= 34(y-1) = Vertical Jump (VJ).
A=A+C A           % A= @StackGrob + 20d + x + 34(y-1).

D0=A              % D0 point to nibble in Row y-1, Column of Nibble x
                  % of the Stack Grob.

C=0 W
A=0 W

*LoadBMap         % Read data from the Stack Grob, Row by Row, and
                  % write it to a new grob.

LA FFC03          % FFC03h= 1111 1111 1100 0000 0011
C=DAT0 A
A=A&C A

C=0 A
C=DAT1 B          % B= 2 nibbles = 8 pixels.

C=C+C A
C=C+C A
C=C!A A
```

```
DAT0=C  A
D0+34              % Next Row of Stack Grob.
D1+2               % Next Row of new grob.
                   % The number of nibbles in a Row is always an even integer.
B=B-1  A           % Decrement the Counter.
GONC LoadBMap



LOAD
D1+15
D+3  A


RPL
ENDCODE
@
```

Exercise: Rewrite the previous code to draw a given 8xN *Sprite* onto the *Screen*. The *Sprite* should be placed at the fourth pixel of nibble x Use FF807h= 1111 1111 1000 0000 0111

Example: Based on the previous examples, write code to draw a given **12** x **N** *Sprite* onto the *Screen*. The *Sprite* should be placed at the second pixel of nibble x.

```
CODE
% This code requires a grob and two binary integers #x, #y on the stack.
% The integers #x, #y indicate the coordinates of a region of
% the Stack Grob where you want to place the grob.
% The #x coordinate is taken from level 2 of the stack, the #y coordinate
% is taken from level 1.
% The grob, given at level 3 of the stack, must be 12 pixels wide but the
% height has no restrictions.
% Warning: Be careful not to write outside the Screen memory.
```

```
SAVE

GOSBVL POP2#        % 2: x ->A.A 1: y ->C.A
R2=C A              % R2= y
R4=A A              % R4= x
                    % Subroutine POP2# updates the RPL Pointers,
                    % and now D1->given grob.


B=C A               % B= y

LC 00022            % Nibbles in a Row of the Stack Grob: 34d=22h
A=0 A               % Cleaning A.A

*Mult               % Calculating at how many nibbles from the origin
                    % of the Coordinate System the Row and the Stack Grob
                    % are found.

B-1 A               % Add 34d, y-1 times.
GOC Cont
A=A+C A
GONC Mult

*Cont
R3=A A              % Save the result in R3

C=DAT1 A            % Address of the given grob.
D1=C                % D1->given grob.
D1+10               % Jump the Pro log
C=DAT1 A            % C= Number of Rows of the given grob
C-1 A               % Adjusting for counting based on Overflow.
B=C A               % Initializing Rows counter of given grob.
D1+10               % D1-> Bitmap of the given grob.

D0=806D5            % D0->ADISP
A=DAT0 A            % A = @StackGrob
LC 00014            % 14h= 20d
A=A+C A             % Skip the Header.
                    % A=@StackGrob +20d

C=R4 A              % C= x = Horizontal jump (HJ)
A=A+C A             % A= @StackGrob + 20d + x
```

```
C=R3 A                % C= 34(y-1) = Vertical Jump (VJ)
A=A+C A               % A= @StackGrob + 20d + x + 34(y-1)

D0=A                  % D0 point to nibble in Row y-1, Column of Nibble x
                      % of the Stack Grob..

C=0 W
A=0 W

*LoadBMap             % Read data from the Stack Grob, Row by Row, and
                      % write it to a new grob.

LA FE001              % FFE01h= 1111 1110 0000 0000 0001
C=DAT0 A
A=A&C A

C=0 A
C=DAT1 X              % X= 3 nibbles = 12 pixels

C=C+C A
C=C!A A

DAT0=C A
D0+34                 % Next Row of Stack Grob.
D1+4                  % Next Row of new grob.
                      % The number of nibbles in a Row is always an even integer.
B=B-1 A               % Decrement the Counter.
GONC LoadBMap


LOAD
D1+15
D+3 A

RPL
ENDCODE
@
```

Note that now D1 is incremented by 4. Although the *Sprite* is only 3 nibbles wide, internally It's encoded with four nibbles, so we need to increment D1 by four to reach the next *Row* data.

Also note that now the padding is larger than in previous examples, since the *Sprite* will have a greater *Width*.

Exercise:
   a) Based on the previous examples, write code to draws a given 16xN *Sprite* on the Screen. The *Sprite* should be placed at the third pixel of nibble x,
   b) Rewrite the previous example to work on the *PICT Grob* with *Right Margin* = 0
   c) Rewrite the previous example to work on the *PICT Grob* with *Right Margin* >0

7.7 Inserting a Sprite into the Screen with x, y coordinates given in pixels.

In the previous sections the "x" coordinate only indicated the nibble of the *Screen* where the *Sprite* was to be placed. In this section, the "x" coordinate will contain more information, since it will refer to the number of the specific pixel, allowing us to know the index of the nibble and the specific pixel within the nibble.

7.8 New Coordinate System.

The *Coordinate System* that we will use from now on is actually the same one we used in the *User RPL*, where the origin of the system is located in the upper left corner of the *Screen*, with coordinates (0,0), and the corresponding coordinates are increased, one by one, as we move to the next pixel to the right and down.

Example: Based on the image on the following page, write the coordinates of each point, and the *Columns of Nibble* where they are located:

1) **A:** *x=2,   y=0,   XN=0*
2) **B:** *x=0,   y=4,   XN=0*
3) **C:** *x=2,   y=4,   XN=0*
4) *E:* *x=7,   y=0,   XN=1*
5) **H:** *x=5,   y=2,   XN=1*
6) **J:** *x=8,   y=5,   XN=2*

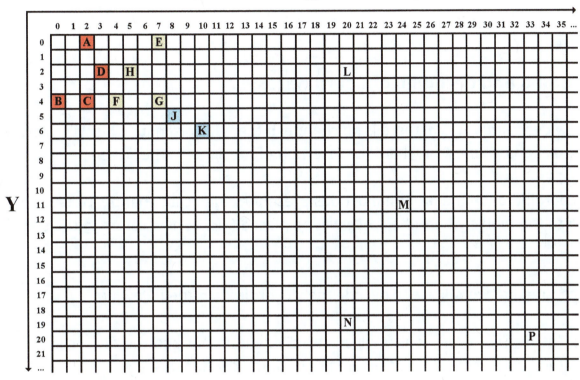

Exercise: Based on the image above, write the coordinates of each point, and the *Column of Nibble* where it is located:

1) D

2) F

3) G

4) K

7.9 Encoding and decoding of Coordinates.

In the new *Coordinate System* there is no change in the "y" coordinate. This will refer, as in the previous sections, to the *Row* where the insertion of the *Sprite* in the *Screen* begins.

The "x" coordinate, on the other hand, does present a significant change, because instead of referring to the nibble where the *Sprite* will be placed (XN), it now refers to the specific pixel (x).

The procedure that we will use to decode the x coordinate is the following:

1) **IntDiv** *Subroutine,* which, given the dividend in A.A and the divisor in C.A, returns the quotient in C.A and the remainder of the division in A.A.

2) The quotient of the division by 4 corresponds to the index of the *Column of Nibble* XN.

3) The remainder of the division corresponds to the index of the pixel column within that nibble, so it will be equal to the necessary shift of the *Sprite bits.* That is:
   a. If the remainder is **zero,** the *Sprite* will be in the **first** column of pixels within the nibble XN.
   b. If the remainder is **one,** the *Sprite* will be in the **second** column of pixels within the nibble XN.
   c. If the remainder is **two,** the *Sprite* will be in the **third** column of pixels within the nibble XN.
   d. If the remainder is **three,** the *Sprite* will be in the **fourth** column of pixels within the nibble XN.

So, we will use the techniques studied in previous sections, about **bitwise shifting** and **logical operations on *Registers*, to place the *Sprite* on** a specific bit of the nibble.

Let's move on to the examples:

Example: Develop a code in *HP Saturn Assembly Language* that takes a *Sprite* of **12** x **N** pixels, and the coordinates "x", "y", and draws the *Sprite* at the given coordinates. The x coordinate is given in pixels, and is supplied as binary integers.

```
CODE
% This code requires a grob and two binary integers #x, #y on the stack.
% The integers #x, #y indicate the coordinates of a region of
% the Stack Grob where you want to place the grob.
% The #x coordinate is taken from level 2 of the stack,
% the #y coordinate is taken from level 1.
% The grob, given at level 3 of the stack, must be 12 pixels wide,
% but the height has no restrictions.
% Warning: Be careful not to write outside the Screen memory.

SAVE

GOSBVL POP2#       % 2: x ->A.A
                   % 1: y ->C.A
R2=C A             % R2= y
R4=A A             % R4= x
                   % Subroutine POP2# updates the RPL Pointers,
                   % and now D1->given grob.


LC 00004
GOSBVL IntDiv      % A.A/C.A= x/4
R4=C A             % R4= Quotient
R1=A A             % R1= Residue


C=R2 A
B=C A              % B= y

LC 00022           % Nibbles in a Row of the Stack Grob: 34d=22h.
A=0 A              % Cleaning A.A

*Mult              % Calculating at how many nibbles from the origin
```

```
                        % of the Coordinate System the Row and the
                        % Stack Grob are found.

B-1 A                   % Add 34d, y-1 times.
GOC Cont
A=A+C A
GONC Mult


*Cont
R3=A A                  % Save the result in R3.

C=DAT1 A                % Address of the given grob.
D1=C                    % D1->given grob.
D1+10                   % Skip the Prolog and Size.
C=DAT1 A                % C= Number of Rows of the given grob.
C-1 A                   % Adjusting for counting based on Overflow.
B=C A                   % Initializing Rows counter of given grob.
D1+10                   % D1-> Bitmap of the given grob.

D0=806D5                % D0->ADISP
A=DAT0 A                % A = @StackGrob

LC 00014                % 14h= 20d
A=A+C A                 % Skip the Header.
                        % A=@StackGrob +20d

C=R4 A                  % C= x = Horizontal jump (HJ).
A=A+C A                 % A= @StackGrob + 20d + x

C=R3 A                  % C= 34(y-1) = Vertical Jump (VJ).
A=A+C A                 % A= @StackGrob + 20d + x + 34(y-1).

D0=A                    % D0 point to nibble in Row y-1, Column of Nibble x
                        % of the Stack Grob..

C=0 W
A=0 W

C=R1 A

C-1 A
```

```
GOC LoadBMap0
C-1 A
GOC LoadBMap1
C-1 A
GOC LoadBMap2
C-1 A
GOC LoadBMap3
```

*LoadBMap0   % Read data from the *Stack Grob, Row* by *Row,*
                       % and write it to
                       % the new grob.
```
LA FF000               % FF000 =1111 1111 0000 0000 0000
C=DAT0 A
A=A&C A

C=0 A
C=DAT1 X               % X= 3nibbles = 12 pixels

C=C!A A
GOSUB UpdPTR
GOTO LoadBMap0
```

*LoadBMap1   % Read data from *Stack Grob, Row* by *Row,*
                       % and write to new grob.
```
LA FE001               % FE001 =1111 1110 0000 0000 0001
C=DAT0 A
A=A&C A

C=0 A
C=DAT1 X               % X= 3nibbles = 12 pixels

C=C+C A
C=C!A A
GOSUB UpdPTR
GOTO LoadBMap1
```

*LoadBMap2   % Read data from the *Stack Grob, Row* by *Row,*
                       % and write it to the new grob.
```
LA FC003               % FC003 =1111 1100 0000 0000 0011
C=DAT0 A
```

```
A=A&C  A

C=0  A
C=DAT1  X          % X= 3nibbles = 12 pixels

C=C+C  A
C=C+C  A
C=C!A  A
GOSUB  UpdPTR
GOTO  LoadBMap2


*LoadBMap3         % Read data from Stack Grob, Row by Row,
                   % and write to new grob.
LA F8007           % F8007 =1111 1000 0000 0000 0111
C=DAT0  A
A=A&C  A

C=0  A
C=DAT1  X          % X= 3nibbles = 12 pixels

C=C+C  A
C=C+C  A
C=C+C  A
C=C!A  A
GOSUB  UpdPTR
GOTO  LoadBMap3


*UpdPTR
DAT0=C  A
D0+34              % Next Row of Stack Grob.
D1+4               % Next Row of new grob.
                   % The number of nibbles in a Row is always an even integer.
B=B-1  A           % Decrement the Counter.
GOC  Exit
RTN
```

```
*Exit

LOAD
D1+15
D+3 A

RPL
ENDCODE
@
```

Note:

This program runs very fast, so to see the result it is recommended to freeze the *Screen* after it runs. You can use a support program that brings the necessary data to the stack, then runs the code and freezes the *Screen* until a key is pressed. You can use something simple like:

```
<< Sprite12 CoordsXY CodeSpr 0 FREEZE >>
```

Exercise:
1) Create a folder named **SPRITEDIR** in the HOME directory of your calculator (or Emulator).
2) Create a 12x15 *Sprite* using the PICT tool in the calculator.
3) Save the *Sprite* from the previous step inside the SPRITEDIR directory and name it **Sprite12.**
4) *System RPL* program that places two binary integers on the stack. For example:

```
::

      BINT9
      BINT1

;
@
```

5) Compile and save the program from the previous step inside the SPRITEDIR directory. Name it **CoordsXY.**
6) Transfer the code from the previous example to your calculator and compile it. Name it **CodeSPr.**
7) Create a small program that calls the *Sprite* onto the stack, then calls the coordinates onto the stack, then runs the code and freezes the *Screen* until a key

is pressed:
```
<< Sprite12 CoordsXY CodeSpr 0 FREEZE >>>
```
8) Save the program from the previous step inside the SPRITEDIR directory. Name it SprExec.

9) Test the code with different values of "x" and "y". Describe the results.

Experimentation

Exploring Memory with the T2 *Experimentation Tool.*

The *Experimentation Tool* T2 also allows you to explore the calculator's memory and view its data graphically, with each bit appearing on the *Screen* as a set or unset pixel.

Some *Graphic Objects* stored in memory can be easily found with this tool. We simply have to move to the memory address where the *Bitmap is,* and the image will appear on the *Screen.*

Experiment 7A: Exploring Memory.

- Start the T2 tool with *a Background Graphic* of 131x80 pixels.
- Use the **[G]** key to point the tool to lower areas of memory.
- You will come across some graphics that will be displayed on the *Screen.*
- Write the results of your exploration in the following table:

Graphic Found	Memory Address (Approximate)	Briefly describe what you observe
1		
2		
3		
4		
5		

You can use the other navigation keys to make jumps of different sizes:

KEY	FUNCTION
X	9 Rows Jump Up
.	9 Rows Jump Down
G	32 Rows Jump Up
J	Jump 32 Rows Down
H	Jump 64 Rows Up
K	Jump 64 Rows Down
Yo	128 Rows Jump Up
L	Jump 128 Rows down
UP	1 Row Jump Up
DOWN	1 Row Jump Down

LEFT	Jump 1 byte up
RIGHT	Jump 1 byte down
ON	Go out

Experiment 7B: Let's find the Meta Kernel Logo.

- Start the T2 tool with *a Background Graphic* of 131x80 pixels.
- Use the large jump keys to move close to the address 63000.
- Use the small and medium jump keys to move close to address 632C0.
- In that *Memory Space* you will find the graphic with the *Meta Kernel* Logo.

Experiment 7C: Let's find the calculator's sources.

- Start the T2 tool with *a Background Graphic* of 131x80 pixels.
- Use the large jump keys to move to address 85000.
- Use the small and medium jump keys to move close to address 851A6.
- Now, press the **[÷]** key until the *Right Margin* value equals **-32,**
- You will be able to see the graphics of the calculator's large fonts (*Big System Font*).
- These sources are located from address 84D82.

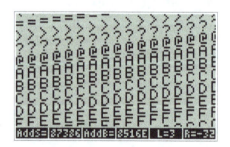

How do you explain the observed repetition of characters on the *Screen?*

CHAPTER 8
VIRTUAL SCREEN

8.1 Virtual Screen.

We can create our own *Screen Grob* to be used instead of the *Stack Grob* or the *PICT Grob*. To do this we must reserve a space in the temporary object area of memory, and supply the address of that space to the *Display Controller,* placing that address in *Register* #00120 (DISP1CTL) of the I/O RAM. With this, the *Controller* will read the data from this new memory address when refreshing the *Screen.*

It's important to note that the *Virtual Screen* must always start at an even memory address. This is because *The System* ignores the least significant bit of the address when reading *Screen* data.

In the original hardware, *The System* reads data in packets of 8 bits at a time, ignoring the least significant bit of memory addresses. This feature is often referred to as byte alignment.

To reserve memory space for our *Virtual Screen* we will use the *Subroutine* "**MAKE$N**", which reserves a string of characters in the temporary objects area, given the number of characters in C.A.

When using MAKE$N we have no control over where the string will be created, so we add an **extra nibble** to the desired size, so that if the string is created at an odd address, we can use the **next even address** as the start of our *Virtual Screen.*

Note:
By setting the reserved space with the structure of an *RPL Object* (a String), we prevent *The System* from reusing that space when performing a *Garbage Collection.*

Example: Write the code to create a *Virtual Screen* of 131 x 80 pixels.

Our *Virtual Screen* will consist of 80 *Rows.* Each of 131 pixels. But, the *Screen* must meet the requirement that the *Row Size* is an integer multiple of eight pixels, since, as we know, the controller works on a byte basis. Therefore:

```
L= CEIL (131/8) bytes= CEIL (16,375) bytes= 17 bytes = 34 nibbles
```

So the total size of the *Bitmap* in nibbles will be:

Zn= 80 x 34 nibbles = 2,720 nibbles

Expressing this number in hexadecimal notation we have:

Zn= AA0h

But, to ensure that we have an even *Start Address*, we will increase this number by 1:

Zn+1= AA1h

```
CODE
%-------------------------------------------------------------------+
% This code creates a Virtual Screen of 80 x 136 pixels.
%-------------------------------------------------------------------+

SAVE                % Save the RPL Pointers.

A=0 W               % Clearing Registers that will be used.
C=0 W

% Create the VirtualScreen:
LC 00AA1            % Set the required size.

GOSBVL MAKE$N       % Create the Virtual Screen (see Entries49, p410).
                    % This routine leaves D0 pointing to the body of the
                    % created string.
                    % (D0->StrBody).

% Set @VirtualScreen:
AD0EX               % Now we have the Bitmap address in A.A
?ABIT=0 0           % Check if it is an even address.
GOYES SetDest       % If odd, add 1 to get the address of the next nibble.
A=A+1 A

*SetDest            % Save the address of the Virtual Screen in R4.
AR4EX W             % [R4= @VirtualScreen ]
```

```
% Register the VirtualScreen:

C=R4 A              % -Copy the address of the VirtualScreen (@VirtualScreen)
                    % in C.A.
D0= 00120           % -Point D0 to DISP1CTL.
DAT0=C A            % -Copy the address (@VirtualScreen) in DISP1CTL.


LOAD
RPL
ENDCODE
@
```

In the previous code we have divided the process into three stages:

1) **Create the *Virtual Screen:*** we load the desired size into C A and execute the MAKE$N *Subroutine*, which leaves D0 pointing to the body of the string. Remember that the structure of a string object is: [*Prolog*] [*Size*] [*Body*].

2) **Set the *Virtual Screen:*** if the address given by MAKE$N is odd, we will use the even address that follows it as the start of our *Virtual Screen.*

3) **We register the *Virtual Screen:*** it consists of telling the *Controller that when* refreshing the *Screen* it should read the data that is in our *VirtualScreen.* This is done by writing the @*VirtualScreen* in the DISP1CTL Exchange *Register:*

   - Copy the address of the *VirtualScreen (@VirtualScreen)* in C.A
   - Point D0 to DISP1CTL.
   - Copy the address *(@VirtualScreen)* in DISP1CTL

After registering the *Virtual Screen,* any changes to your data will appear on the physical *Screen* of the calculator.

Exercise: Compile and run the code above. Describe your observations. How can we explain what is displayed on the *Screen?*

8.2 Drawing Sprites on a Virtual Screen.

Handling *Sprites* in the *Virtual Screen* is similar to what we did in previous sections with the *Stack Grob* and *PICT Grob*. We simply use a *Pointer Register* to point to the *Sprites,* and another to point to the *Virtual Screen.* We read and copy the data and increment the *Pointers* to the next *Rows*.

Let's see an example:

Example: Rewrite the example from the previous section to draw a *Sprite* of 8x10 pixels, on the *Virtual Screen.* The *Sprite* is given on the stack. The coordinates will be x=0, y=0 by default.

```
CODE

%------------------------------------------------------------------+
% This code creates a Virtual Screen of 80 x 136 pixels.
%------------------------------------------------------------------+

SAVE              % Save the RPL Pointers.

A=0 W             % Clearing Registers that will be used.
C=0 W

% Create the VirtualScreen:
LC 00AA1          % Set the required size.

GOSBVL MAKE$N     % Create the Virtual Screen (see Entries49, p410).
                  % This routine leaves D0 pointing to the body of
                  % the created string.
                  % (D0->StrBody).

% Set @VirtualScreen:
AD0EX             % Now we have the Bitmap address in A.A
?ABIT=0 0         % Check if it is an even address.
GOYES SetDest     % If it is odd, we add 1 to obtain the address of the
                  % next nibble.
A=A+1 A
```

```
*SetDest             % Save the address of the Virtual Screen in R4.
AR4EX W              % [R4= @VirtualScreen].

% Register the VirtualScreen:

C=R4 A               % -Copy the address of the VirtualScreen
                     % (@VirtualScreen) in C.A.
D0= 00120            % -Point D0 to DISP1CTL.
DAT0=C A             % -Copy the address (@VirtualScreen) in DISP1CTL.

D0=C                 % D0 point to the Virtual Screen.

LC 0A                % Registering Sprite Row Counter.
B=C B
B-1 B                % Setting counter for loop exit when Overflow.

C=DAT1 A             % We have the Sprite at level one of the stack.
D1=C
D1+10
D1+10                % D1 point to Sprite Bitmap.

*LoadRow

A=DAT1 B             % Read a Row from the Sprite.
DAT0=A B             % Copy Sprite Row to Virtual Screen.
D1+2                 % Jump to the next Row of the Sprite.
D0+34                % Jump to the next Row of the Virtual Screen.
B-1 B                % Decrement Rows Counter.
GONC LoadRow

LOAD
RPL
ENDCODE
@
```

Example: Write a code to generates a *Virtual Screen* from a given grob on the stack.

```
CODE
%--------------------------------------------------------------------+
% This code creates a Virtual Screen from a given grob.
% Requires a grob at level 1 of the stack. We will call this
% grob the "Background"
%--------------------------------------------------------------------+


SAVE                % Save the RPL Pointers.


% Create VirtualScreen ------------------------------------------+


                    % This VirtualScreen will have the same dimensions as
                    % the graphic given at level 1 of the stack.


% Collecting Background Information:
A=0 W               % Clearing Registers that will be used.
C=0 W


C=DAT1 A            % Save @Background in R1.
CR1EX W             % [R1= @Background]


A=DAT1 A            % Accessing the Background grob.
D0=A                % Applying Indirection.


D0=D0+5             % Read the size of the Background grob (SizeBackgroundGrob).
A=DAT0 A
A=A-15 A            % Calculate the size of your Bitmap.


% (SizeBackgroundBMap= SizeBackgroundGrob-5-5-5).
AR2EX W             % Save the size of the Bitmap in R2.
                    % [R2= SizeBackgroundBMap]
D0=D0+15            % Point D0 to the Background Bitmap (BackgroundBMap).
                    % (We are moving forward)
AD0EX               % Save the address of the Bitmap (@BackgroundBMap) in R3.
AR3EX W             % [R3= @BackgroundBMap]


% Create the VirtualScreen:
                    % The Virtual Screen is a string.
                    % in temporary memory, to which we can write and read
                    % data. To create it we will use the ML routine "MAKE$N",
                    % which requires us to indicate the size of the string
                    % in C.A.
```

```
C=R2 A              % Set the required size:
C=C+1 A             % An extra nibble is added to ensure Parity
% of the address.
                    % Explaining: The data of a Virtual Screen must start
                    % at an even memory address. This is necessary
                    % due to certain hardware restrictions  of the calculator.
                    % When using MAKE$N we have no control over where the
                    % string will be created, so we add an extra nibble, such
                    % that, if the string is created at an odd address,
                    % we can make use of the next even address.


GOSBVL MAKE$N       % Create the Virtual Screen, of a size equal to the
                    % Background  (see Entries49, p410)
                    % This routine leaves D0 pointing to the body of the
                    % created string.
                    % (D0->StrBody)
                    % Remember: The structure of a string object:
                    % [ Prolog ][ Size ][ Body ]


% Set @VirtualScreen:
AD0EX               % If the address given by MAKE$N is odd,
                    % we will use the next even address.
?ABIT=0 0           % If it is even, we jump to SetDesc, which will save
                    % the address in R4.
GOYES SetDest       % If odd, we will use the address of the next nibble
                    % than if it is at an even address.
A=A+1 A             % Add 1 to get the address of the next nibble.

*SetDest            % Save the address of the Virtual Screen in R4.
AR4EX W             % [R4= @VirtualScreen ]

% Copying Bitmap of the Background to the VirtualScreen: -----------------+
                    % For this we will use the MOVEDOWN routine,
                    % which requires:
                    % -Number of nibbles:   C.A
                    % -Data source:         D0
                    % -Data destination:    D1


C=R2 A              % The number of nibbles to be copied is equal to
                    % the Size of  Background.


A=R3 A              % The Origin is the Background Bitmap (BackgroundBMap),
                    % whose address is in R3.

AD0EX
```

```
A=R4 A              % The Destination is the VirtualScreen (VirtualScreen),
                    % whose address is in R4.
AD1EX

GOSBVL MOVEDOWN     % Execute MOVEDOWN to copy C A nibbles from
                    % address D0 to address D1.


% Register the VirtualScreen:
                    % It consists of telling the controller that when refreshing
                    % the Screen must read the data that is in our VirtualScreen.
                    % This is done by writing the @VirtualScreen to the Register
                    % DISP1CTL exchange:
C=R4 A              % -Copy the address of the VirtualScreen (@VirtualScreen)
                    % in C.A
D0= 00120           % -Point D0 to DISP1CTL.
DAT0=C A            % -Copy the address (@VirtualScreen) in DISP1CTL.

                    % Now, any modification to the VirtualScreen data
                    % will appear on the Real Screen.

LOAD
RPL
ENDCODE
@
```

Exercise: Based on the previous example,

  a) Write a program to creates a *Virtual Screen* of 131 x 64 pixels.
  b) Write a program to creates a *Virtual Screen*, given its *Width* and *Height* on the stack as two binary integers.

CHAPTER 9
THE MENU

9.1 The Menu.

At the bottom of the *Screen* there is the calculator's menu bar. This important interactive component allows the user quick and easy access to different System options, and is often a very useful resource for programmers.

From the perspective of graphical programming, a great advantage of the menu is that it has an independent graphic (*Menu Grob*), so we can disable or modify it without affecting the other graphical spaces (*PICT Grob* and *Stack Grob*).

The *Menu Grob* address can be found in the VDISP2 *Register,* located at address 806D0 in the I/O RAM.

The address of the menu *Bitmap* can be read in 80695 (DISP2CTLg), the *Ghost Register* of #00130 (DISP2CTL) used by the *Display Controller.*

Registers		DESCRIPTION
Address	Name	
00130	DISP2CTL	Contains the address of the *Bitmap* used by the *Display Controller to know* which pixels in the *Menu Area* or *Secondary Area* of the *Screen* should be set and unset. It is a write-only *Register,* so its contents cannot be accessed directly.
80695	DISP2CTLg	Contains a copy of the contents of DISP2CTL that we can access. It is sometimes named the *Ghost Register* of DISP2CTL.

9.2 Drawing a custom grob in the Menu Area.

To assign a custom graphic to the *Menu Area,* simply supply the *Bitmap* address of the new grob to the *Display Controller* by placing that address in the DISP2CTL *Register* (00130).

The *Menu Area* requires a fixed-size graphic of 131x8 pixels, meaning it has **8 Rows**, and each *Row* must have a *Size of* **17 bytes** (36 nibbles). When *The System* refreshes the *Screen* of the *Menu Area,* sometimes named *Secondary Area,* the sum of the *Right Margin* and the *Left Margin* is disabled, so the *Display Pointer* cannot be offset if a *Graphic Object with* other dimensions is used.

Example: Write a code to takes a 131x8 pixel graphic, given at level 1 of the stack, and draws it in the *Menu Area*.

```
CODE
SAVE
A=DAT1  A
LC 00014              % 14h = 20d
A=A+C  A
D0=00130
DAT0=A  A

LOAD
RPL
ENDCODE
@
```

You can restore the screen to its normal state by restarting the machine with ON+C.

The above method requires that the graphic given on the stack be at an **even memory address** in order to be displayed properly, since *The System* ignores the least significant bit of the memory address when reading the data.

Another method is to create a *Virtual Screen,* which allows the programmer to guarantee the placement of data at an even address.

9.3 Virtual Screen for the Menu.

Just as we created a *Virtual Screen* for the *Main Area of the Screen,* we can create a *Virtual Screen* for the *Menu Area.*

Example: Write the code to create a *Virtual Screen* for the menu.

The Virtual Screen requires 8 *Rows for the menu,* each of 131 pixels. But, the *Screen* must meet the requirement that its *Width* or *Rows Size* be an integer multiple of eight pixels, since, as we know, the controller works based on bytes. Therefore:

```
L= CEIL (131/8) bytes= CEIL (16,375) bytes= 17 bytes = 34 nibbles
```

So the total size of the *Bitmap* in nibbles will be:

Zn= 8 x 34 nibbles = 272 nibbles

Expressing this number in hexadecimal notation we have:

Zn= 110h

But, to ensure that we have an even Start Address, we will increase this number by 1:

Zn+1= 111h

```
CODE
%-----------------------------------------------------------------+
% This code creates a Virtual Screen for the menu of 8 x 136 pixels.
%-----------------------------------------------------------------+

SAVE                % Save the RPL Pointers

A=0 W               % Clearing Registers that will be used
C=0 W

% Create the Virtual Screen for Menu:
LC 00111            % Set the required size.

GOSBVL MAKE$N       % Create the Virtual Screen (see Entries49, p410).
                    % This routine leaves D0 pointing to the body of
                    % the created string.
                    % (D0→StrBody).

% Set @VirtualScreen:
AD0EX               % Now we have the Bitmap address in A.A.
?ABIT=0 0           % Check if it is an even address.
GOYES SetDest       % If odd, add 1 to get the address of the next nibble.
A=A+1 A

*SetDest            % Save the address of the Virtual Screen in R4.
AR4EX W             % [R4= @VirtualScreen ].

% Register the VirtualScreen:
```

```
C=R4 A              % -Copy the address of the VirtualScreen
                    % (@VirtualScreen) in C.A.
D0= 00130           % -Point D0 to DISP1CTL.
DAT0=C A            % -Copy the address (@VirtualScreen) in DISP1CTL.

LOAD
RPL
ENDCODE
@
```

If we run the above code, we will see the *Menu Area* filled with random, meaningless data. This is because we haven't write anything into the *Virtual Screen yet*. You can reset the calculator by doing ON-C to return the menu to its default state.

We can modify the code from the previous example to draw a grob on the *Virtual Screen*.

Example: Rewrite the code from the previous example so that it draws a 131x8 *Graphic Object,* given in the *Stack,* on the *Virtual Screen* before registering it.

```
CODE
%-----------------------------------------------------------------+
% This code creates a Virtual Screen of 8 x 136 pixels for the menu.
% Then copies a given grob onto the stack in the Virtual Screen,
% and sets the Virtual Screen as the menu graphic.
%-----------------------------------------------------------------+

SAVE                % Save the RPL Pointers.

A=0 W               % Clearing Registers that will be used.
C=0 W

% Create the Virtual Screen for Menu:
LC 00111            % Set the required size.

GOSBVL MAKE$N       % Create the Virtual Screen (see Entries49, p410).
                    % This routine leaves D0 pointing to the body of the
                    % created string.
                    % (D0->StrBody).
```

168

```
% Set @VirtualScreen:
AD0EX              % Now we have the Bitmap address in A.A.
?ABIT=0 0          % Check if it is an even address.
GOYES SetDest      % If odd, add 1 to get the address of the next nibble.
A=A+1 A


*SetDest           % Save the address of the Virtual Screen in R4.
AR4EX W            % [R4= @VirtualScreen ].

% Copy Stack Grob to Virtual Screen:
A=DAT1 A
D1=A
D1+10
D1+10
LC 11              % 272 nibble/16 = 17 cycles = 11h cycles.
C-1 B              % Setting to exit when Overflow occurs
B=C B              % Row Counter


C=R4 A
D0=C


*Load16N
C=DAT1 W
DAT0=C W
D1+16
D0+16
B-1 B
GONC Load16N


% Register the VirtualScreen:


C=R4 A             % -Copy the address of the VirtualScreen
                   % (@VirtualScreen) in C.A
D0= 00130          % -Point D0 to DISP1CTL.
DAT0=C A           % -Copy the address (@VirtualScreen) in DISP1CTL


LOAD
RPL
ENDCODE
@
```

The grob given in the stack has 8 *Rows* of 34 nibbles each, giving a total of 272 nibbles, which are copied to the *Virtual Screen* in 17 packets of 16 nibbles.

$$272/16 = \mathbf{17} \qquad\qquad (\text{this is } \mathbf{11h} \text{ in hexadecimal})$$

To be able to use the GONC *Instruction* appropriately, we had to decrement the counter by 1, so that the *Overflow* is generated at 17 cycles of the Load16N loop.

Exercise: Use the PICT environment on your calculator to create a *Graphic Object* of 131x8 pixels. Then use the above program to set it as a graphic for the menu.

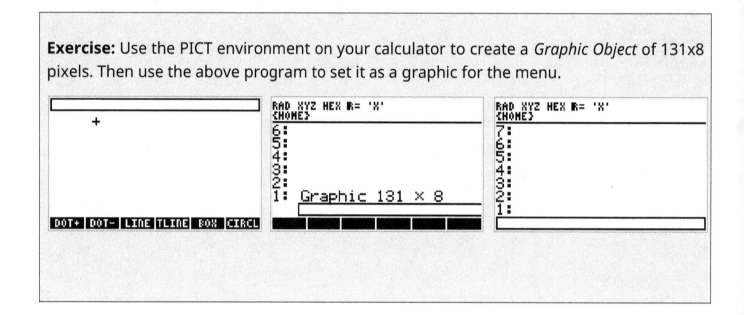

9.4 Drawing a custom label in the Menu Area.

The *Menu Area* usually has six labels, each 21x8 pixels, and *Columns* of 1x8 pixels separating each pair of labels.

There are different types of labels:
- Standard label.
- Menu label.
- Directory label.
- Inverted label.

```
▒▒▒▒▒▒▒ CALCULATOR MODES ▒▒▒▒▒▒▒
Operating Mode..RPN
Number Format....Std              _FM,
Angle Measure....Radians
Coord System......Rectangular
 ✓Beep   _Key Click  ✓Last Stack



Choose calculator operating mode
FLAGS CHOOS  CAS  DISP CANCL  OK
```

FLAGS CHOOS CAS DISP CANCL OK

Experimentation
The Lines Counter
(HP49G, HP49G+ and HP50G)

In this section we will use the *Experimentation Tool* T1.

On the HP 50G, the default value for the *Lines Counter* or LINECOUNT is 55d. Increasing the value of this variable causes the menu to move to the bottom of the *Screen* until it disappears. When LINECOUNT reaches the value 63, the menu has completely disappeared.

On the HP50G we can continue to increase the *Lines Counter* beyond the previous value without any observed glitches. When its value is greater than 65d an apparent vertical rotation of the data occurs, causing the menu to now be displayed at the top of the *Screen,* and continue to scroll down as the *Lines Counter* is increased further.

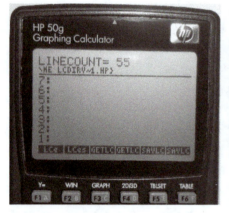
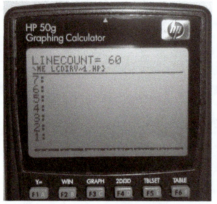
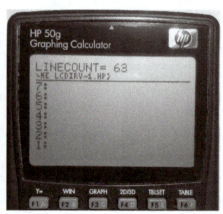

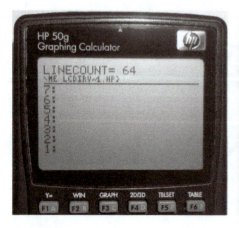
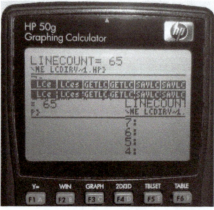

By reducing the *Lines Counter* value, the menu appears shifted upwards. The minimum value it can take with the menu still visible is 1:

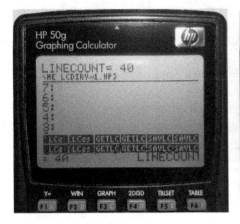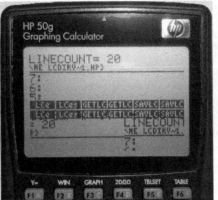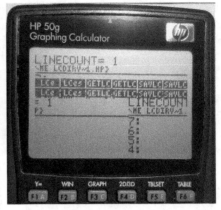

When the *Lines Counter* is equal to zero, the menu disappears:

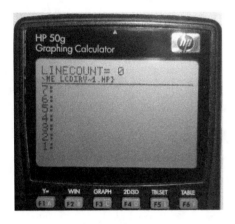

The HP 49G has a similar behavior to the HP 50G: the default value for the *Lines Counter* is also 55d. When you increase the value of this variable, the menu moves to the bottom of the *Screen* until it disappears. When LINECOUNT reaches the value 63, the menu has completely disappeared.

On the HP 49G, if we continue to increase the *Lines Counter* beyond the previous value, the *Screen* goes blank, and this does not change with higher values. On the 49G, the data rotation that we see on the 50G does not occur.

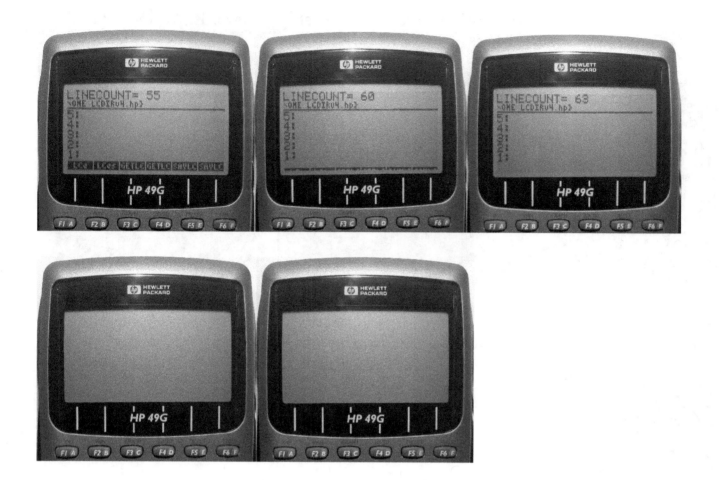

By reducing the *Lines Counter* value, the menu appears shifted upwards, just like on the HP 50G, and the minimum value it can take with the menu still visible is 1:

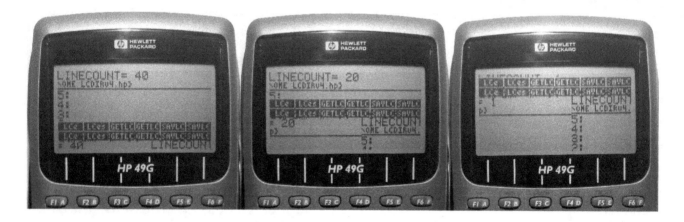

When the *Lines Counter* is equal to zero, the menu disappears, just like on the 50G:

Warning!

Avoid values greater than 63 on the HP 48 and 49G. If you notice any errors, press the ON key to exit the program and turn the calculator off and on again.

Experimentation Tool Keyboard

KEY	FUNCTION
-	Decrease LINECOUNT by 1
+	Increment LINECOUNT by 1
÷	Reduce LINECOUNT by 8
x	Increase LINECOUNT by 8
0	Makes LINECOUNT = 0
1	Makes LINECOUNT = 10
2	Makes LINECOUNT = 20
3	Makes LINECOUNT = 30
4	Makes LINECOUNT = 40
5	Makes LINECOUNT = 50
6	Makes LINECOUNT = 60
7	Makes LINECOUNT = 70
8	Makes LINECOUNT = 80
9	Makes LINECOUNT = 90
Other	Go out

CHAPTER 10
DISPLAY CONTRAST

10.1 Display Contrast.

The contrast is encoded by five bits at address #00101 of the *I/O RAM*.

Address	Bit 3	Bit 2	Bit 1	Bit 0
#00101				
#00102				

With these five bits we can have up to 32 different contrast values, showing the *Screen* darker as the value in these bits is increased.

When working with these *Registers*, care must be taken not to affect the other bits at address #00102. In the following example we will work with only the first nibble, so we will not change the value of the most significant bit of the contrast:

Example: Write a code to increase the contrast by one unit:

```
CODE
SAVE
D0=00101

A=DAT0 B          % xxxy yyyy
A=A+1 P           % xxxy YYYY
                  % We assume that P=0.
DAT0=A B

LOAD
RPL
ENDCODE
@
```

If instead of increasing the contrast, we want to reduce it, we simply subtract instead of adding:

```
CODE
SAVE
D0=00101

A=DAT0 B          % xxxy yyyy
A=A-1 P           % xxxy YYYY
```

```
                        % We assume that P=0.
DAT0=A B

LOAD
RPL
ENDCODE
@
```

The above codes have several limitations:
- The range of possible values for contrast is reduced to just 16, since we only manipulate one nibble of the *Register.*
- The contrast obtained will depend on the value previously held in the fifth bit of the *Register.*

10.2 Using the fifth bit of contrast.

We can improve our code by also using the fifth bit of the contrast. When doing so, we must be careful not to modify the other bits of the nibble. To do this, we will use a mask that allows us to place the new value of the contrast while keeping the rest of the bits unchanged. Let's see this:

Example: Write a code to increase the contrast, using the five available bits and keeping the other bits unchanged in the second nibble.

```
CODE
SAVE
D0=00101

LC 1F              % 0001 1111
B=C B

A=DAT0 B           % xxxy yyyy
A+1 B
A=A&B B            % 000Y YYYY

LC E0              % 1110 0000
B=C B
```

```
C=DAT0 B      % xxxy yyyy
C=C&B B       % xxx0 0000

C=C!A B       % xxxY YYYY

DAT0=C B

LOAD
RPL
ENDCODE
@
```

We can easily modify the above code to reduce the contrast instead of increasing it:

```
CODE
SAVE
D0=00101

LC 1F              % 0001 1111
B=C B
A=DAT0 B           % xxxy yyyy
A-1 B
A=A&B B            % 000Y YYYY

LC E0              % 1110 0000
B=C B

C=DAT0 B           % xxxy yyyy
C=C&B B            % xxx0 0000

C=C!A B            % xxxY YYYY

DAT0=C B

LOAD
RPL
ENDCODE
@
```

180

10.3 Adjust the contrast by a specified amoun.

What if we want our code to increase the contrast by a specific value?

Example: Write code to adjust the contrast by a specified amount. The increment value will be passed on the stack's level 1 as a binary integer.

```
CODE

SAVE

GOSBVL  POP#        % # -> A.A

D0=00101
C=DAT0  B           % xxxy yyyy
C=C+A  B            % XXXY YYYY

LA  1F              % 0001 1111
A=A&C  B            % 000Y YYYY

LC  E0              % 1110 0000
B=C  B

C=DAT0  B           % xxxy yyyy
C=C&B  B            % xxx0 0000

C=C!A  B            % xxxY YYYY

DAT0=C  B
LOAD
RPL
ENDCODE
@
```

Exercise: Rewrite the code from the previous example to reduce the contrast instead of increasing it. Transfer both codes to your calculator (or emulator) and test how they work with different contrast values.

10.4 Loading a specific contrast value.

What if, instead of increasing or decreasing the contrast, we want to assign it a specific value?

Example: Implement a routine to adjust the contrast to a given level. The routine will retrieve a binary integer from the stack representing the desired contrast and set the contrast accordingly.

```
    CODE

    SAVE

    GOSBVL POP#      % # -> A.A

    LC 1F            % 0001 1111
    A=A&C B          % 000Y YYYY
    LC E0            % 1110 0000
    B=C B

    D0=00101
    C=DAT0 B         % xxxy yyyy
    C=C&B B          % xxx0 0000

    C=C!A B          % xxxY YYYY

    DAT0=C B

    LOAD
    RPL
    ENDCODE
    @
```

Exercise: Develop software in *HP Saturn Assembly Language* to displays a bar with the contrast level, and that allows you to change its value.

CHAPTER 11
GRAYSCALE GRAPHICS

11.1 Grayscale Graphics.

Starting with the HP 49G, *The System* includes new resources for working with *Grayscale* images. These include new *System RPL* commands, dedicated *Memory Areas* for this type of graphic, and an *Interrupt Service Routine* that enables a special display mode using these more sophisticated graphics.

11.2 How do Grayscale Graphics work?

The *Graphic Object* represents images using a binary system: each pixel is either set (1) or unset (0). This binary representation limits the *Display* to two colors. *Grayscale* is achieved by rapidly toggling each pixel between these two states, creating the illusion of intermediate shades. A pixel that is set for a longer period will appear darker on the *Screen*.

To create this effect, the calculator rapidly switches between multiple *Graphic Objects* of identical dimensions. This switching occurs at such a high speed that the eye cannot perceive the individual frames. A pixel's state can vary across these alternating graphics, leading to different *Shades of Gray*. A pixel that is unset in all the alternating graphics will appear unset on the *Screen*.

If for example we alternate successively the following three graphs:

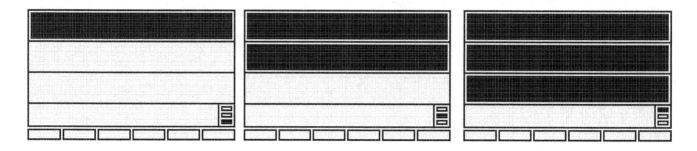

The uppermost rectangle will be displayed in a dark shade, since its pixels are set in each one of the alternating graphic frames. The rectangle below it will be slightly less dark, because its pixels are only set in two out of the three graphic frames. The third rectangle down will appear brighter than the two above it. The lowermost rectangle will be shown in the lightest possible shade, as its pixels are not set in any of the three graphic frames.

So, if we alternate between three different graphics, we can get four different *Shades of Gray:*

GROB	SHADES			
	100 %	66%	33%	0%
1	Set	Set	Set	Clear
2	Set	Set	Clear	Clear
3	Set	Clear	Clear	Clear

11.3 Specific memory areas for Grayscale Graphics.

Starting with the HP 49G, special memory areas are available that can be used by programmers to work with *Grayscale Graphics.* These areas are located between memory addresses 822B2 and 84D6E (where 844EE+880). In this space it is possible to store several *Graphic Objects*, so that we can then alternate them to generate the *Grayscale effect* on the *Screen.*

11.4 Memory Space distribution in the HP49G.

The HP 49G has a resolution of 136x64 pixels (34x64 nibbles), the *Memory Space* available between addresses 822B2 and 84D6E is large enough to contain up to five *Graphic Objects* the size of your *Screen:*

    Grob 1: #8229Eh
    Grob 2: #82B32h
    Grob 3: #833C6h
    Grob 4: #83C5Ah
    Grob 5: #844EEh

Each grob will take up 20+ (34x64) nibbles = 20+2176 nibbles = 2196 nibbles = #894h nibbles

The first 20 nibbles at each address in the above list will be occupied by the *Header* of each *Graphic Object* (*Header: Prolog + Size + Height + Width*). Therefore, the *Bitmaps* of each graphic will be located at the following addresses:

    Screen 1: 8229Eh + 14h = #822B2h
    Screen 2: 82B32h + 14h = #82B46h
    Screen 3: 833C6h + 14h = #833DAh
    Screen 4: 83C5Ah + 14h = #83C6Eh

```
        Screen 5: 844EEh + 14h = #84502h
```

Note that all of these addresses are even.

It is important to mention that the first of these spaces is used by the *Operating System* to store the *Command Line* graphic (ECRAN), so it may be convenient for the programmer to only use the graphic spaces after this one.

Note also that the last 272 nibbles of each space (#110h) correspond to a menu area, that is, 8 *Rows* of 34 nibbles each.

11.5 memory Space distribution in the HP 50G.

As we know, the 50G has a larger *Screen* than the 49G. A full *Screen* on the 50G requires:

20 + 34x80 nibbles = 2740 nibbles = #AB4h nibbles

As a result, the *Memory Space* layout will be different:
```
        Grob 1: #8229Eh
        Grob 2: #82C2Eh
        Grob 3: #836E2h
        Grob 4: #84196h
```

For the *Bitmaps* of each graphic above, we will have:

```
        Grob 1: #8229Eh + 14h = #822B2h
        Grob 2: #82C2Eh + 14h = #82C42h
        Grob 3: #836E2h + 14h = #836F6h
        Grob 4: #84196h + 14h = #841AAh
```

As in 49g, the first space is used by the *Operating System* for the *Command Line*, so it is recommended to use only spaces 2, 3, and 4.

Note that with this memory allocation, there is still some unused space, but it is not enough to hold the data for a full *Screen*. However, it can be used by the programmer for other purposes.

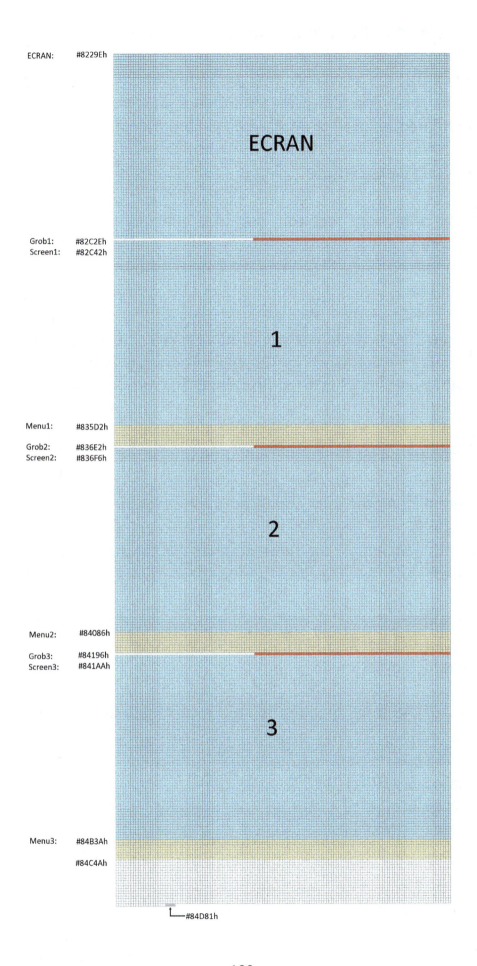

ECRAN: #8229Eh

ECRAN

Grob1:   #82C2Eh
Screen1:   #82C42h

1

Menu1:   #835D2h

Grob2:   #836E2h
Screen2:   #836F6h

2

Menu2:   #84086h

Grob3:   #84196h
Screen3:   #841AAh

3

Menu3:   #84B3Ah

              #84C4Ah

#84D81h

11.6 Using the Interrupt Service Routine for Grayscale Graphics.

When a *Interrupt* occurs, the calculator's CPU jumps to address #0000Fh, where the *Interrupt Handler* is located. This important program includes a *Subroutine* for *Grayscale Graphics*, which can be configured, enabled or disabled by the programmer.

What exactly does this *Subroutine* do?

When enabled, this subroutine creates a grayscale effect by rapidly cycling through three graphics on the screen.

How do you activate it?

The *Interrupt Handler* checks the first nibble at address 8069C (GreyOn?), and if it finds a non-zero value, it activates the *Subsystem* for *Grayscale*. Therefore, to activate this *Subsystem*, we simply need to set a non-zero value in the first nibble at address 8069C.

What does this *Subsystem* need?

You need three graphics for the stack and three graphics for the menu.

The addresses of the *Bitmaps* of the three graphics for the stack must be supplied at the following addresses:

```
#8069Dh  named  GreyScr1
#806A7h  named  GreyScr2
#806B1h  named  GreyScr3
```

Bitmap addresses of the three graphics for the menu must be supplied at the following addresses:

```
#806A2h  named  GreySoft1
#806ACh  named  GreySoft2
#806B6h  named  GreySoft3
```

11.7 General Procedure:

a) **PreLoad:** Copy the graphics data to the addresses Grob2, Grob3 and Grob4.
b) **SetScreen:** Set the GreyScr1, GreyScr2 and GreyScr3 stack area.
c) **SetMenu:** Configure the GreySoft1, GreySoft2 and GreySoft3 menu area.
d) **TurnGreyOn:** Enable the *Subsystem* for *Grayscale* (GreyOn? > 0).
e) Press a key to generate an *Interrupt*.

Example: Write a program to uses the *Subsystem* for *Grayscale* on the HP 50G.

The program will be splitted into several modules:

Module1 PreLoad: Requires three 131 x 80 pixel *Graphic Objects* at stack levels 1, 2, and 3.

```
CODE
SAVE

D0=82C2E
GOSUB LoadGn

D0=836E2
GOSUB LoadGn

D0=84196
GOSUB LoadGn

GOTO Exit


*LoadGn

AD1EX
R1=A A
D1=A

A=DAT1 A
D1=A        % Applying Indirection to point to the grob data.

LC 000AB
%C-1 A
```

```
        *LoopX

        A=DAT1 W
        DAT0=A W
        D0+16
        D1+16
        C-1 A
        GONC LoopX

        A=R1 A
        AD1EX
        D1+5

        RTN

        *Exit

        LOAD
        RPL
        ENDCODE
        @
```

Module2 SetScreen:

```
        CODE
        SAVE

        LA 82C42
        D1=8069D
        DAT1=A A

        LA 836F6
        D1=806A7
        DAT1=A A

        LA 841AA
        D1=806B1
        DAT1=A A

        LOAD
        RPL
```

```
ENDCODE
@
```

Module3 SetMenu:

```
CODE
SAVE

LA 835D2
D1=806A2
DAT1=A  A

LA 84086
D1=806BC
DAT1=A  A

LA 84B3A
D1=806B6
DAT1=A  A

LOAD
RPL
ENDCODE
@
```

Module4 TurnGrayOn:

```
CODE
SAVE

D0=8069C
LA 01
DAT0=A  P

LOAD
RPL
ENDCODE
@
```

Module5 TurnGrayOff: Allows you to deactivate the *Subsystem.*

```
CODE
SAVE

D0=8069C
LA 00
DAT0=A P

LOAD
RPL
ENDCODE
@
```

We will use the following graphs, which we will save in the variables G1, G2 and G3:

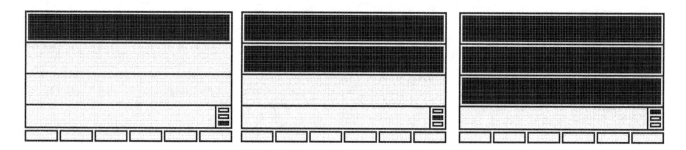

We can create a sixth module to run all the previous modules in sequence.

Module 6 ExGray:

```
«
CLLCD
G3 G2 G1
PreLoad SetScreen SetMenu
3 DROPN
TurnGreyOn
»
```

To disable the *Subsystem*, run TurnGreyOff or restart the calculator with ON-C.

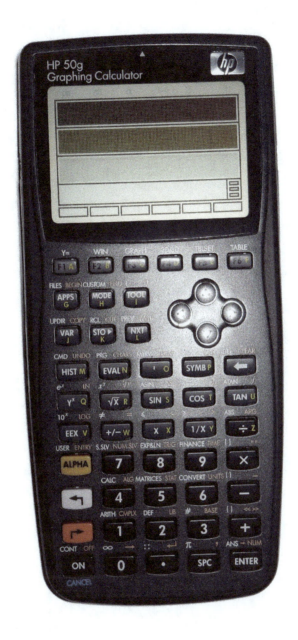

APPENDIX

EXPLORING THE INSIDE OF THE SYSTEM

I. The First Journey.

This *System* works so well! It would be interesting to open it up and see what those brilliant people who designed it have put inside.

But, to do that I need a special tool. I can use this one named "Nosy", a software to converts all those hexadecimal codes to a language closer to human: The *Assembly Language.*

So, using that sophisticated tool, I begin my exploration of the intricate *System*. The place I select to start is address #0000F, where I know a very important routine named *Interrupt Handler* is located.

I point the tool at that mysterious location in the machine's memory and the exploration begins!

There I find a lot of *instructions* that are a bit confusing at first, but little by little they start to make sense. The code jumps from one place to another continuously and sometimes it becomes difficult to follow.

This is a little discouraging, but I have an idea: how about drawing a diagram to help me follow the code as I read it?

I start drawing a flowchart, which serves as a map to find the point from which the jumps occur. The diagram turned out to be an excellent idea!

I'm finding a lot of interesting stuff during my journey, and I can identify areas dedicated to very specific functions: One to handle the keyboard, another for timers and alarms, others for the transmit and receive ports (UART). There's one that checks if the battery is low, and if so, it alerts the user about the problem. There's even one to manage the cursor on the *Screen* when we type. If an error is detected, the routine jumps to an area where the machine is reset (Warm Start).

At address 001BE I found something very strange... The tool shows me the code BUSCC, followed by the operational code D2. The BUSCC code was supposed to be discontinued since the HP 48.

After a brief investigation I found out that the HP 50G has *Instructions* that did not exist in the 48, and for these new *Instructions* they used the code BUSCC followed by other digits.

The powerful Nosy tool fails when it encounters these new codes and cannot read them correctly. Nosy fails to believe that these are two separate *Instructions*, when in fact it is just a new operation code resulting from the combination of BUSCC (80B) and some other complementary digits.

Many of these new operating codes remain a mystery today.

II. Where is the RTI?

Several days have passed since my first exploration trip into the depths of this complex *System*, where I found many interesting things; something common in this kind of adventures.

Today I make my second foray, with the goal of plotting a route to the exit.

Those flowcharts I drew when I was first here are now a very valuable resource.

...

I can pay more attention to certain details, such as the mechanisms for backing up the CPU *Registers* at the beginning of the *Interrupt Handler* code to compact P, Carry, Arithmetic mode, and Sticky into a 5-bit package at address 805EB. That other bit there is simply a zero.

I am also struck by the segmentation of the C *Register* into two parts, each stored in a different location.

Immediately after this I find something really cool:

An area where I can redirect the flow of execution to my own code so that *The System* executes it by itself, without my intervention. This area is named "*User Interrupt 1*".

To start this last custom code, *The System* compares two different addresses, and if they have the same content, the corresponding *Subsystem* is activated.

...

Later, at address 0014A, another surprise: a *Subsystem* for handling *Grayscale Graphics* begins to be seen.

I proceed cautiously, knowing that a single lapse in concentration could lead me get lost in this complex labyrinth.

Suddenly, the manager of the big clock: the TIMER2.

Its mechanisms are activated with two requirements (11AC and 11B3): INT=1 and SREQ=1

I tell to myself: The alarm controls must be there!

...

I was right, here they are!
...

As the reader will understand, this journey requires significant effort and focus.

I still haven't been able to find the way out and I'm already starting to feel a little exhausted.

Although many areas are easy to identify, because they manipulate Control *Registers* whose I/O RAM addresses are well known to programmers, at this point I have the feeling that *The System* is refusing to reveal its secrets to me.

...

I pause for a moment and look at the diagram I've been drawing.
Rojo
I realize that 1C3 and 1CF and 1D8 are all leading me in the same direction.

So I decide to explore that area of memory....

It was a good decision! The second and final "*User Interrupt*" is here. Now I know that the exit must be close!

[The nice thing about *User Interrupt* 2 is that by using it you no longer have to worry about modifying the CPU *Registers,* because at this point *The System* already has a backup of all the CPU *Registers*, which you can restore by jumping to address 23F].

As often happens, the simplest answer ends up being the correct one.

I stop at the fork in the road heading 23A, look carefully, and I can see a small light in the distance. I walk to it and finally, after a long journey, I find myself right at the exit of the complex labyrinth, unmistakably identified by the *Instruction* "RTI".

END

Thank you for joining me on this journey!

LEARN MORE:
      Nosy: https://www.hpcalc.org/details/4323
      New opcodes: https://www.hpcalc.org/details/6259
      Interrupt Handler: https://sites.google.com/view/mnavarrodocs/home